GETTING YOUR START IN HOLLYWOOD

Steve Sagman

GETTING YOUR
START
IN
HOLLYWOOD

◆

Copyright ©1991 by Steve Sagman

Peachpit Press
2414 Sixth St.
Berkeley, CA 94710

ISBN 0-938151-51-7

0 9 8 7 6 5 4 3 2 1
Printed and bound in the United States of America

DEDICATION

◆

For Sabina, our own leading lady.

CAST OF CHARACTERS

◆

ED SEDARBAUM
Editor

MILTON ZELMAN
Editor

SANDRA SHAP
Silhouettes

ACKNOWLEDGMENTS

◆

My great thanks go to two special individuals at IBM Desktop Software for their enthusiastic support of this project: Chris Clow, Senior Business Planner, and Ivan Ruiz, Program Manager for Hollywood. Though busy bringing Hollywood to life, they always found the time during the development of this book to lend an ear or offer a special insight.

Thanks also to Ed Holcomb and the folks at Publishing Solutions, Inc. for dreaming up such a wonderful product, and to Gary Vieregger, IBM Technical Support Manager, for fielding my constant questions.

I also want to gratefully acknowledge the invaluable contributions of three very talented people: Ed Sedarbaum, for his intricate editing, Milton Zelman, for his consummate art direction, and Sandra Shap for the charming illustrations you'll find at the beginning of each chapter. And really, how could I have done it without Eric and Lola?

CHAPTERS

◆

SETTING THE SCENE
Getting to Know Hollywood

SCREEN TEST
Auditioning Hollywood

THE SCREENPLAY
Outlining a Presentation

THE LEADING ROLES
Adding Bullet and Data Charts

THE SUPPORTING PLAYERS
Adding Table and Tree Charts

TITLES AND CREDITS
Working with Text

IMAGE MAKING
Drawing in Hollywood

BEHIND THE SCENES
Using Preferences, Color Schemes, and Templates

ROLL 'EM!
Producing Screen Shows

THE BIG PREMIERE
Producing Output

EXTRAS

CONTENTS

THE SUPPORTING PLAYERS: *Adding Table and Tree Charts*

TITLES AND CREDITS: *Working with Text*

IMAGE MAKING: *Drawing in Hollywood*

BEHIND THE SCENES: *Using Color Schemes, Templates, and Preferences*

ROLL 'EM!: *Producing Screen Shows*

THE BIG PREMIERE: *Producing Output*

EXTRAS

SETTING THE SCENE

Before You Begin

In This Chapter

◆

What Is Hollywood?

Have you always dreamt of making it big in Hollywood? Here's your chance. What will it be? A big-box-office slide show? A fast-moving, action-packed on-screen presentation? Or a dignified documentary for the board of directors?

IBM's exciting new presentation graphics program for Windows makes you the director of your own major Hollywood features. And because it works in the Windows environment, it's easy to use. Like a director peering through the lens, you'll always see on the screen exactly what your presentation will look like when it's finally on slides, overheads, or printed pages.

The Plot Unfolds

When you start Hollywood, you'll be looking at the first blank page of a new presentation. Over on the left is Hollywood's Toolbox, filled with tools for creating everything you make in Hollywood. Need a pie chart? Pull a Pie Chart tool from the Data Charts drawer. Need to draw freehand? Grab the Paintbrush tool from the Paint drawer. Want to organize your thoughts first? Good idea. In Hollywood's Outliner, you can plot out a presentation and organize its sequence of topics; Hollywood will automatically transform your outline into a series of bullet charts. And if you've left a little space on the page for a graph, a table, or an organization chart, you can drop one of those in place next. Of course, you'll find tools for each of them in the Toolbox, too.

For the Picasso in You

Dazzling charts and graphs are just the beginning, though. In Hollywood's Toolbox, you'll also find tools for drawing shapes and painting designs: everything the artist in you craves. Perhaps it's a logo for your letterhead that you need, or a special design for a presentation's background. With Hollywood's tools, you'll create it easily.

But if the thought of actually drawing on the screen scares you, then you can borrow liberally from Hollywood's Graphic Library. It's filled with dozens of predrawn clip art images. You'll even find complete chart designs for you to use; just take a walk through Hollywood's Chart Gallery.

Then, when you've just about finished your presentation, you can summon up miniature "thumbnail" versions of its pages in Hollywood's Presentation View. There you can slide them from position to position, changing their order in the presentation, or you can leap from there right to any single page you still want to work on.

Production Design

With other presentation graphics programs, it's your job to make sure that the style of every slide in your

---

In Hollywood, what you see on the screen is what you'll get on paper, overhead transparencies, and 35mm slides.

Hollywood is automatic enough for the casual user and sophisticated enough for the graphics professional.

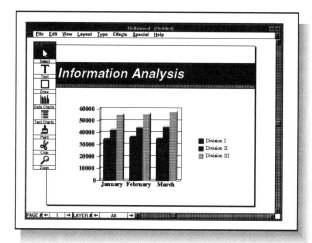

*The Main Presentation
Window of Hollywood*

presentation matches all the others. But in Hollywood, a template does that *for* you. Load a template when you start a presentation, and you'll get just the presentation background you like, and just the chart designs you want. The template always works behind the scenes designing the objects you make with each tool. Use the Line Chart tool to enter the numbers for a line chart, and the template will design the line chart for you and place it on the page just right.

Where do you get templates? Some come with Hollywood, but you can make your own, too. Any presentation you've custom designed can be saved as a template. Load it up in the future and it will design other presentations the same way.

For the Hitchcock in You

Not content with a staid series of slides? A drab printed handout? Or commonplace black-and-white overheads? Why not let Hollywood turn your presentation into an animated show right on the screen? Each new page can erupt into view with a dazzling video-like special effect, fading up, wiping in from the left, or even flashing onto the screen in a lightning bolt. Or let Hollywood dramatically build your text and graph charts right before your audience's eyes. Each new thought you present in a bulleted line of text can emerge brightly as the ones you've already covered recede into the background. Or, when you're ready, each new pie slice can join the ones already assembled into a three-dimensional pie.

And these are only the highlights — just a hint of what Hollywood is capable of. Think of this book as your Hollywood tour guide, leading you carefully and patiently through everything this wonderful program can do. ★

Using This Book

Because *Getting Your Start in Hollywood* has been designed to introduce to you Hollywood in the shortest possible time, it's been laid out a little differently from most computer books. Here's how.

Each time you turn the page, you'll be revealing a new topic, laid out neatly from beginning to end in a two-page spread. Exactly what you need to know about a particular Hollywood feature is right there in front of you. No more. No less.

This book is composed of eighty-five of these neat, self-contained little spreads grouped into eleven chapters. Every spread that you finish is another significant step on your road to Hollywood success.

Follow the Hands-on Approach

You'll probably find that you can read through a spread in a matter of minutes. You might even be tempted to read through a series of them without trying the steps each spread recommends. If you're familiar with Windows programs and presentation graphics software, you may be able to get by with this approach. If you're not (and that makes you the very person this book was written for), try this instead: Read about it, do it, and then read about it again. You'll gain greater insight into the material after you've used Hollywood hands-on. Plus, trying a procedure yourself will probably raise a few questions that you'll find answered when you reread the same spread.

Don't overlook the carefully captioned pictures. Wherever a picture details a series of sequential steps, you'll find the steps numbered. And don't overlook the comments in the left margin of each spread, either. Usually they extract the choicest morsels from the text, or add a tip or trick you'll want to know about.

If you're already using Hollywood and only need to learn about a particular feature or just refresh your memory, you can jump right to its spread. There's a detailed table of contents at the front of the book and a thorough index at the back to help you navigate. But really this book is meant for the Hollywood newcomer.

What You'll Learn When

When you're ready to begin exploring Hollywood, the next chapter will take you on a guided Hollywood tour, introducing you to the most significant parts of the program. You'll be placed in a real scenario and be given a real presentation to create; that way you'll learn a few of the guiding principles that should help you throughout the rest of the book. Then, in the following chapter, you'll hear about the Outliner and how it's used to organize a presentation and create the presentation's basic pages.

Once you've got a series of pages, you'll try adding to them charts of all types: colorful and expressive graph charts; informative table and organization charts. Next, you'll

▼

Place this book right next to the keyboard and try everything it recommends. It's the best way to learn.

▼

When you finish a two-page spread, you can be confident that you've learned everything about a topic that you need to know.

discover how to add separate text and special graphics to your pages, whether to enhance their beauty or to make them more communicative. You'll also learn about the special tools Hollywood provides; these can take over the work of designing the presentation, leaving you free to concentrate on its content instead.

Finally, you'll learn how to debut your presentations before the general public: by printing pages, by making slides, or by producing full-fledged screen shows. The last chapter is reserved for special topics you'll want to come back to after you've mastered the Hollywood basics: tips and tricks, finetuning touches, and a special guide for those who'll be helping others to use Hollywood.

At the end of each chapter you'll find a "Where To from Here?" box. They measure your progress, show everything you've mastered, and give you a sense of where you are in the material. You'll see one of these boxes right on this page.

Windows Experience Will Help

Although the instructions in this book always tell you exactly how to use Hollywood's menus, dialog boxes, pull-down lists, and other controls, you may find it easier to learn Hollywood if you already have a little Windows experience under your belt. All Windows programs work alike. But if Windows is brand new to you, I'd recommend *The Little Windows Book*, by Kay Nelson. Published by Peachpit Press (800-283-9444), the same company that publishes this book, it's a delightful, concise introduction to using Windows.

Finally, no matter what any book claims, no book can help you master a powerful piece of software "in a matter of minutes." A computer program can be learned through the pages of a book, with the over-the-shoulder guidance of a friend, or in a classroom, but you won't really master any program until you've worked with it for a while, developing your own special techniques.

Ready to begin? Okay. Quiet on the set! ★

Where To from Here?

Outlining the Presentation
Adding Bullet and Data
  Charts
Adding Other Chart Types
Adding the Trimmings: Extra
  Text and Graphics
Formatting the Presentation
Showing Off Your Work

Your Hollywood career begins with picking up a little background. In the next few pages you'll get that background — a couple things of you'll need to know before embarking on a short Hollywood tour, also contained in the next chapter.

SCREEN TEST

Auditioning Hollywood

In This Chapter

◆

Hollywood's Feature Is the Presentation

Software for making individual charts and graphs has been around almost as long as the personal computer. But programs that design an entire presentation with many charts and graphs are still new. So new, in fact, that Hollywood is one of the first.

Outline Organizing

What's so great about the fact that Hollywood lets you work on an entire presentation at one time? With the full presentation in your sights, you can easily adjust how ideas flow from one page to the next.

The tool Hollywood provides for this, the *Outliner*, lets you create a presentation by creating an outline for it. The outline is a list of main topics, each followed by comments you've made about that topic.

Now, nothing can force you to think through the order of a presentation, but Hollywood gives you a gentle nudge in that direction by giving you the tools to reorganize those topics until you've got a clean, coherent sequence that gradually builds to an inescapable conclusion.

From Outline to Pages

When the presentation outline is complete, a single command instructs Hollywood to turn the outline into a series of presentation pages. Obediently, Hollywood turns each main topic into a page title and places it on a new page; your comments become text items below the title.

Your presentation has become a series of pages you can browse through in the main Hollywood window.

Now you can head off and do some work on the individual pages, refining the text and adding graphic charts, perhaps. Or, you can jump into Presentation View and see little thumbnail representations of each page that you can slide around on the screen, in effect rearranging your presentation. Sound easy? It is. But only because Hollywood lets you organize the content of your presentation as a unit — as a series of unified pages — rather than hammering out one chart at a time, as you might have done in old-fashioned presentation graphics programs.

Total Makeovers

Working with an entire presentation at once offers other advantages, as well. Chief among them is that you can change your presentation's overall appearance as easily as you can its content, making just a few alterations that affect every page simultaneously. This ensures a unity of design, and makes your work not only easier to understand but more professional looking. Your presentation looks custom designed rather than thrown together from bits and pieces you happened to have lying around.

In Hollywood, the device that dictates a consistent look throughout a presentation is called a *color scheme*. Because your presentation has a color

---

▼

Hollywood focuses its lens on entire presentations, not just individual charts and graphs.

▼

The presentation outline holds the structure of the presentation: the sequence of its pages.

▼

You can work on individual charts and graphs, or you can work on the entire presentation just as easily.

scheme, all page titles get a specific color and type size, for instance, and all bullet charts get bullet points of the same color. But these are just a few examples. Changing the color scheme will change the design of all similar objects on every page.

A Familiar Echo

Developing all the pages of a presentation in a single file rather than in separate files also makes it easy to place a graphic logo or picture on every page. Having the same graphic on every page creates a familiar echo your audience learns to identify with. Perhaps it's your company or division logo, a piece of clip art that pertains to the topic, a photo of the team mascot, or your own picture added for grace and elegance. Any graphic placed on Hollywood's *Master Page* instantly shows up on every page, just as if you'd copied it from one page to the next.

Keeping It All Together

Finally, storing all of the pages of a presentation in the same file on disk makes them easy to find again and to retrieve. And it makes them easy to move to another disk or archive onto a floppy disk for long-term storage.

Simply put, working on an entire presentation is much better than working on individual charts, and nearly all of these benefits come from three principal tools Hollywood gives you: the Outliner, color schemes, and the Master Page. The rest of this chapter gives you a little better idea how these key Hollywood components work together with the rest of Hollywood's tools and commands. Later in the book, you'll find separate chapters telling you everything you need to know about actually using them. ★

The Rest of This Chapter

The next several pages introduce a number of key Hollywood concepts. Some are easy and straightforward and others are the kind you'll need to experience before you'll fully understand. Don't worry if you don't grasp them at first. Later in this chapter you'll be taking a guided Hollywood tour to get some hands-on experience with Hollywood's tools and menus. Of course, later in the book, you'll be learning in detail about each of the concepts you first become acquainted with here. That's where things should really pull together.

A Presentation's First Cornerstone: The Outliner

Hollywood's ability to plan and design an entire presentation, not just individual charts, rests on three cornerstones: the Outliner, color schemes, and the Master Page. Let's take a look at each of these separately.

Cornerstone One: The Outliner

The Hollywood Outliner shows up in its own window when you summon it to organize the sequence of messages your presentation will deliver. Usually, this is when you begin thinking seriously about the presentation's content.

In the Outliner, you start by typing a preliminary list of topics. (They're preliminary because you can always change the list and add more later.) Then, you arrange and rearrange the list until you're impressed with how logically and cleverly it proceeds from one topic to the next.

Of course, your topics *might* occur to you in perfect, logical order, but most of us need to brainstorm a bunch of ideas first and then sort and resort them until they're properly sequenced. Whether or not you make use of the organizing powers of the Outliner, you'll still need the Outliner to create bulleted text charts, as you'll see.

Words or Numbers?

Once you've got a list of topics in the Outliner, you can evaluate the story each one tells and determine how best to communicate it. Some ideas come across better through words in a text chart; others involve numbers that cry out to be represented in a graphic chart. Under each "words" topic, you enter an indented list of comments you'd like to make. These will soon become bulleted text items on a presentation page. Under the "numbers" topics, you enter nothing; that leaves the space beneath the page title clear so you can add a graphic chart later.

Creating the Pages

Now, when you give the signal (the Draw Chart command), Hollywood scans down your outline and creates a separate presentation page for each main topic it finds. Each topic automatically appears on its page as a title. Any comments you've indented under a main topic will be placed on the page, too, but as a list of bulleted text items underneath the page title. If you've entered *several* levels of indented text (second-level items followed by third-level items, etc.), Hollywood places them all on the page in the same indented pattern.

▼

Drawing charts from the Outliner creates your presentation pages.

▼

The Outliner is always available for you to reorganize a presentation.

▼

You must return to the Outliner to make changes to the content of bullet charts.

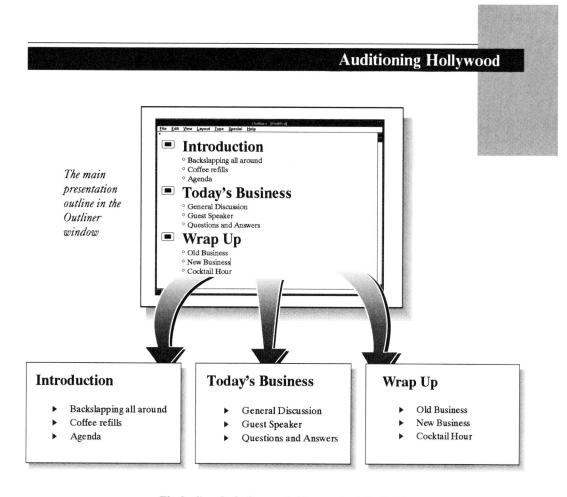

The main presentation outline in the Outliner window

The Outliner Is the Source of a Presentation's Bullet Charts

That's how you get an entire presentation of bulleted text charts. You simply enter into the outline a list of page titles with indented comments underneath each. Hollywood takes care of turning them all into bullet charts. Of course, if you haven't entered anything under a page title in the outline, Hollywood puts a page title on the page, but leaves the rest of the space on that page clear so that later you can add a graphic data chart, organization chart, or table chart.

The Outliner is also helpful for editing a presentation. By returning to the outline after viewing an individual page, you can insert new topics and comments and delete or edit others. In fact, you *must* return to the outline to make changes to any of the page titles or bulleted text points. Then, when you use the Draw Chart command again, Hollywood creates a new, revised set of pages. ★

Cornerstones Two and Three: The Master Page and the Color Scheme

Hollywood's Outliner helps design the *content* of a presentation. Hollywood's two other cornerstones, the Master Page and color schemes, help design a presentation's *look*.

Cornerstone Two: The Master Page

Any graphic object you place on the Master Page — a logo in the corner, say, or a patterned background — will appear on every single page of your presentation, and in the identical spot on the page. That's how graphics and designs on the Master Page add uniformity to a presentation.

Using the Master Page lets you quickly tailor your work to a specific audience, perhaps by adding a potential client's logo to the corner of each page.

Cornerstone Three: The Color Scheme

Every presentation has a color scheme — nothing more than a list of design rules, really, covering each separate category of item in a presentation. One design rule, for example, makes every page title a certain size, typeface, and color. Another specifies the color that will fill every object you draw with one of the Draw tools — until you select a different color. And so on.

A color scheme will have a different set of rules for each different type of text chart, plus another set of rules covering all data charts, the background page, and any objects placed on top of the background page. Because color schemes apply a

▼

The Master Page and the color scheme help design the look of a presentation.

▼

You can place any graphic object on the Master Page, and select any of the available color schemes or design your own.

Master Page

Presentation Pages

A Graphic Placed on the Master Page Appears on All Pages.

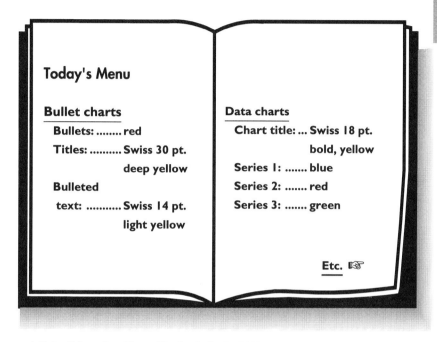

A Color Scheme Is a Menu of Design Rules for Different Objects in a Presentation

particular style of formatting all the way through a presentation, they, like the Master Page, also help create uniformity in a presentation.

Another benefit of color schemes is instant conversion. Say you've got a very colorful presentation designed (via its color scheme) specially for 35mm slides. Suddenly you need to print it out — but on a black-and-white laser printer. There's no need to redo the presentation. Just change the color scheme to one with only shades of gray and in no time you're up and running — with a presentation redesigned to suit a different output device.

Where do you get color schemes? A starter set, created by professional designers, comes built in to Hollywood, but you can change these color schemes, inventing your own combinations of colors and other attributes, and then save your changes as new and even better color schemes. You'll learn the nitty-gritty of modifying and saving color schemes in Chapter 8. In fact, you'll learn the details of all three of Hollywood's cornerstone components later in this book. ★

Hollywood's Convenience Controls

Preferences and Templates take a lot of the work out of using Hollywood.

U sing the Outliner and a color scheme are fundamental to building a clear, consistent presentation, and the Master Page can add some unifying graphics. Two more Hollywood components, preferences and templates, serve a very different purpose: They can make your work much more convenient.

Preferences

Selecting a preference file arranges Hollywood just the way you like it, with its windows laid out just so and its Toolbox filled with just the tools you'll need, set exactly the way you like to use them. This alone is enough to make a preference file valuable, but it does still more.

A preference file also designates a page size and orientation (horizontal or vertical) that suits the output device you'll be using, and a color scheme that's appropriate for the output device, too. Because the color scheme the preference file specifies makes most of the design choices for your presentation, you're free to concentrate on entering the presentation's content. You end up with a presentation that requires only a few finishing flourishes.

Hollywood comes with a handful of preference files optimized for different types of output devices. Every time Hollywood starts up, the preference file used last gets loaded once again — but you can select any

Preferences set up Hollywood the way you like and templates set up your presentations the way you like.

other preference file before beginning a new presentation. Perhaps you'd like a preference file that's optimized for a 35mm slide presentation, or one that's best for a series of overheads you'll print on a laser printer. Choosing a different preference file is simply a matter of selecting one from the list you see when you use the Preferences command.

Creating your own preference files is just as easy. Once you've got Hollywood operating just the way you want, you use the Preferences command to save that operating state into a file. Now, any time you load the same preference file, Hollywood reverts instantly to the saved state.

Hollywood is so customizable that it's good to know there's an easy way to save each useful configuration.

Templates

Just as a preference file is a way to recall a complete operating status of Hollywood, a template is a way to recall a complete presentation design you've created, right down to the positions of charts on pages.

A template holds a record of each different page design in your saved presentation. It also remembers the color scheme applied to that presentation and how the individual charts and graphic objects look (determined by what's called their "options" settings). To give an existing presentation a completely

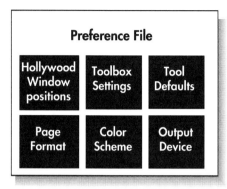
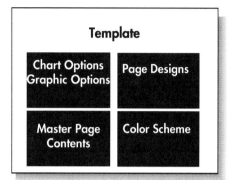

The Preference File and Template Store Important Hollywood Settings

different design, you can try applying a different template to it. This will come in handy when you have several different output devices. You can create templates that are optimized for each device. ★

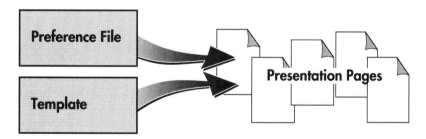

How Preference Files, Color Schemes, and Templates Work Together

Preference files, color schemes, and templates are interrelated. Here's how they relate:

The preference file determines which color scheme a new presentation will use. Once you've started the new presentation, you can change its color scheme to give its objects different designs (different colors, fill patterns, line styles, and text fonts).

You can also apply a template to a presentation, changing the color scheme plus a whole lot more: the position of the charts and titles on the pages, and the options settings that control the look of individual charts and graphic objects.

Attaching a template makes more design changes than you get by simply changing the color scheme, but a change of color scheme is often enough to give a presentation a vastly different appearance.

Hollywood's Tools, Menus, and Dialog Boxes

A deceptively straightforward statement of fact: In Hollywood, everything you create is an object placed on a page.

Obvious, right? Yes, and simple too. But the concept is so fundamental, so basic to working with Hollywood, that you must get it like religion before you go on to start up the program. For example...

Every object you place on a Hollywood page belongs to one of two groups: some are text and some are graphics. Think of a bullet chart. It's composed of two objects, both of them text: a title object (that's the page title, which used to be a main topic in your outline) and a sub-titles object (all the bulleted points under the title are actually a single object). And each graphic shape you draw in Hollywood is also a separate object: draw three rectangles on the Hollywood screen and you've got three rectangle objects. A data chart, such as a pie chart or a line chart, is also one object.

Adding Objects with Tools

To add an object to a page, you use the tools that Hollywood keeps grouped by category in the Toolbox. One drawer of the Toolbox, labeled "Draw," holds all the tools you need for drawing graphic objects (lines, boxes, circles, polygons, and so on). Another drawer, labeled "Data Charts," holds all the tools for

creating data chart objects (pie charts, line charts, column charts, and so on). A third drawer, labeled "Text Charts," holds tools for creating the three different types of text charts (bullet charts, table charts, and tree charts). Each text chart is composed of several objects.

You'll find the Toolbox over on the left side of the Hollywood screen. It has eight drawers, each one with a handle labeled with its name, plus a faceplate that shows the most recently selected tool. To look inside a draw for a tool, click on one of the drawer handles with the mouse. For example, click on the handle labeled "Data Charts" to open the Data Charts drawer and reveal all the tools inside.

Editing Objects with Menu Commands

Once you've added an object to a presentation page with a tool, you may want to modify it using one of Hollywood's many menu commands. First, select the object by clicking once somewhere in the middle of it (you can tell an object has been selected because small black handles appear around it). Next, select a

Most charts are composed of several objects, but a data chart is a single object.

You can modify the appearance of objects using menu commands or the object's options.

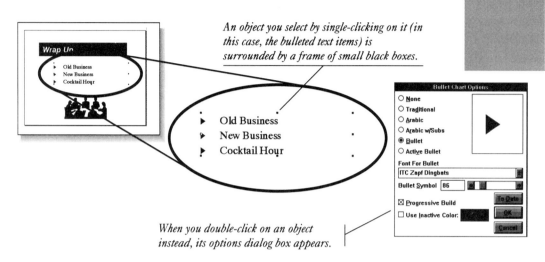

An object you select by single-clicking on it (in this case, the bulleted text items) is surrounded by a frame of small black boxes.

When you double-click on an object instead, its options dialog box appears.

menu command to modify it. To use a Hollywood menu, click on one of its words (for example, click on Effects) and then select a command from the menu you've pulled down.

Exercising Your Options

Most objects also have a set of controls, called "options," that adjust particular aspects of their appearance. To change the options of an object, double-click on the object to summon its options dialog box, and then make changes to the controls within the

box. Any changes you make to these options will have an immediate effect on the appearance of the object.

In short, objects can be added to pages using the tools in Hollywood's Toolbox. Then you click on an object to select it and use a menu command to modify it. Or you can double-click on an object to bring up its modifiable options in a dialog box. Changes made in an options dialog box affect only the chart you're currently working on. ★

How Do I Know When to Change an Object's Options?

How do you know whether to try to change the look of an object by using a menu choice or by using the object's options? Here's the difference: Hollywood's menus hold commands you can use to modify any object. You can change the color of any object, so there's a command called Colors on the Effects

menu. The options dialog box for an object (double-click on the object to get it) holds only aspects of the object that are unique to that object type. Data charts have an option to change the scaling of their axes, for example. Bullet charts have an option to change the shape of the graphic bullet. And so on.

Taking a Hollywood Tour

So far, the descriptions in this chapter have been abstract. You've had to imagine how the various pieces of Hollywood fit together without actually seeing them. Now it's time to join a Hollywood tour, where you'll get the chance to try firsthand a few of the tools, menu commands, and options dialog boxes in a "real" scenario. There's no better way to learn.

From here on out in this chapter, you'll take a guided Hollywood tour.

Imagine...

Imagine yourself, for the purposes of this tour, as one of the many head-office minions at the studios of famed motion picture mogul Harry Geld, Jr. Harry himself has called on you to prepare a brief presentation promoting his latest brainstorm: *Lola: Terror In Her Cards*.

Here are the topics Harry wants to present:

By the time you've finished the tour, you'll have seen enough of Hollywood to get a good sense of how the program works.

1. The idea for the picture: Lola, a clairvoyant trained in Hungary, foretells the year 2000 and is pursued by the CIA, MI-5, and the KGB.
2. Harry's estimates of viewing-audience interest, by region, in a major motion picture about a clairvoyant who finds herself in one harrowing scrape after another.
3. Harry's ideas for several lucrative movie tie-ins.

Prior Planning Pays

After gathering specific information from Harry, you settle in with Hollywood and begin. What you'll want to do is create three presentation pages. Three pages wouldn't really make much of an impact in a formal presentation — you'd probably want to throw in a whole bunch of supporting material as well — but this is just a sample to show Harry.

The first and last pages will have bullet charts, but the middle one needs to have a data chart: Harry's numeric projections, you've decided, can best be represented in a bar chart.

To create the three pages, you'll start with Hollywood's Outliner and enter the presentation text for all three charts. For the middle chart, you'll type into the Outliner only the title. Then, you'll have Hollywood draw the charts. Onto the middle chart — which so far has nothing but a title — you'll drop your data chart. On the Master Page, you'll place a logo for the presentation, something or another about Lola (you'll figure that part our later). And finally, you'll experiment a little with color schemes to get just the look you want. Maybe you'll even try applying a template or two to the presentation to see if an entirely different format might work even better. By the time you've done all this, you should have a pretty good

To Do

1. Gather Information
2. Start Hollywood and check preference file
3. Enter list of topics into Outliner
4. Enter comments about first and last topic
5. Use Draw Chart to generate pages
6. Go to second page and start data chart
7. Enter data into Data Manager
8. Use Draw Chart to generate the chart
9. Modify chart's options, if necessary
10. Use Master Page for repeating graphic
11. Print the chart

Your Checklist

idea of how all Hollywood's pieces fit together.

Starting Hollywood

If you haven't already started Hollywood, now is the time to do it. Double-click on the star icon in the Hollywood window inside the Program Manager. In a few moments, Hollywood will appear full screen.

Before you proceed, you should check a few settings to be sure they're OK; someone else may have used the Hollywood you're now working with and changed its default settings. The first place to check is the program's preferences settings. That's covered next. ★

Starting a Presentation

Hollywood keeps track of the way the program was last set up by recording it in a preference file. Each time you start Hollywood, it loads the preference file that was used last. Because the settings in the preference file will affect how your presentation appears, it's important to check that the correct one is loaded before you start a new presentation.

Checking Preferences

First, select Preferences... on the File menu. Up pops the Preferences dialog box, displaying the currently loaded preference file in a text box on the left. Pressing the button just to the right of the text box pulls open a list of existing preference files. Today you'll be creating charts to display on the computer screen, so you should select Screen Show.

Normally, when you're working in Hollywood, selecting a preference file from the list is all you need to do — if there's one already set up to your liking. But let's take a look at the settings in the preference file by selecting the button labeled More.

Now you can see that a preference file holds six sets of settings: Page Format, On Startup Load, Color Scheme, Pages Per Handout, Measurement, and Output Device.

For the purposes of this tour, make sure that Page Format is set to Screen, Color Scheme is set to Screen Show/VGA, and Output Device is set to None. Press the button next to each of these controls to pull down the list of available choices and then click one of these choices. You can leave all the other settings in this dialog box as is. Then select OK.

Now that you've selected a preference file, you're ready to begin a new presentation by selecting New (for a new presentation) on the File menu. Yes, that is a blank page you see on the screen even before selecting New. And yes, it is indeed the first page of a blank presentation. But you still must select New because that blank page is still under the jurisdiction of the *old* preference file. The presentation you create after selecting New will use the preference file settings you just established. The new presentation is set up for the screen and has the Screen Show/VGA color scheme attached, as you specified in the preference file. As you add charts and objects, they'll be automatically formatted by the Screen Show/VGA color scheme. You'll see.

Check to see which preference file is active before starting a new presentation. It will set up Hollywood a certain way.

The same preference file always loads when you start Hollywood until you select a different one.

File	
New	Ctrl+N
Open...	Ctrl+O
Close	
Save...	Ctrl+S
Export Page As...	
Import Picture...	
Import Text...	
Preferences...	
Page Setup...	
Change Printer...	
Print...	Ctrl+P
Exit	

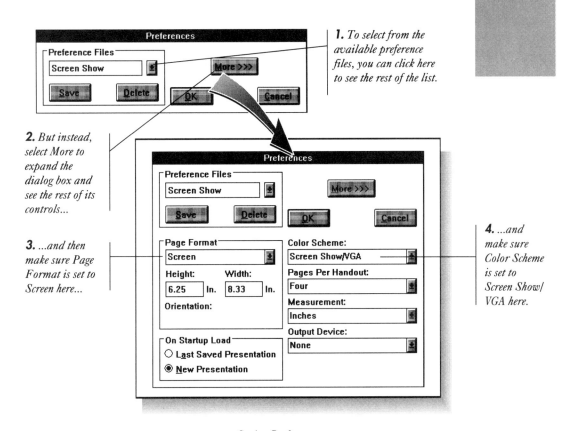

Setting Preferences

Summoning the Outliner

To begin entering the content of the presentation, you'll need to summon the Outliner window. Go to 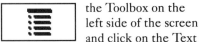 the Toolbox on the left side of the screen and click on the Text Charts drawer. Inside, you'll find all the tools you need to create text charts. Since bullet charts are created directly from the presentation outline, click on the Bullet Chart tool. It's the first of the three tools in the Text

Charts drawer, and it looks like a little bullet chart.

In a flash, the Outliner window opens up, with "Outliner - (Untitled)" at the top. (The Outliner window also opens when you start a tree chart, since the structure of a tree chart gets entered in outline form.) Now you're ready to enter the three main topics in Harry's presentation, as well as the comments that will become bulleted text points. Exactly how to do that comes next. ★

Creating the Presentation Outline

In the upper left corner of the Outliner window you'll see a small dot with a double frame below it. The cursor is somewhere to the right of the double frame. That double frame represents the first page of your presentation. You're all set to enter text onto it, so start typing your first topic, "Lola's Prophesies for the Year 2000," and then press Enter.

The text you've just typed is fairly long and its left end is pushed up against the double frame. Later, when you generate actual presentation pages from this outline, you'll see that the text on the final pages (the page titles and the bulleted lines below) looks exactly like the text back in the Outliner — same typefaces, same alignment.

Because you pressed Enter at the end of the main topic, the cursor is now on the line below. To enter the first of the subordinate comments, press Tab once; this indents the cursor one level to the right. Now type in the three phrases you see in the sample outline on the facing page. Press Enter after each.

When the comments for the first topic are all in place, press Shift-Tab to move the cursor to the left once again, back to the page-title level, and type the next main topic. Continue following this scheme (Tab to indent to the right, Shift-Tab to move back left) until you've entirely duplicated the sample outline.

Manipulating the Outline

Once the outline is complete, try double-clicking on the line marker (the double frame) at the left end of the first main topic. Notice that the comments underneath it temporarily disappear. This lets you hide extraneous detail while you're reorganizing a presentation. To return the hidden comments to view, double-click on the same line marker again. Other techniques in the Outliner let you rearrange the order of topics and subtopics and copy them from place to place.

In this case, though, the outline you've just finished needs no changes, so you're ready to generate presentation pages using the Draw Chart command on the File menu.

Generating the Presentation Pages

When you use Draw Chart, you'll be taken immediately to a single page of your presentation. Now you're looking at the real thing: your presentation just as Harry will see it (unless you decide to modify it — which you will). To turn from page to page so you can inspect all three pages, click on the arrow that's just to the right of the page number at the bottom of the presentation window. To return to the previous page, click on the left arrow instead. Sure enough, you'll see that all three pages of the presentation display the text from the outline: main topics as page titles and comments as subordinate text points.

▼

All the text in the presentation outline will show up in bullet charts.

▼

The Outliner shows text exactly as it will appear in bullet charts — same typefaces, same alignment.

After entering the first line...

...press Tab to indent to this second level...

...and press Shift-Tab to return to the first level.

Line marker

Entering the Presentation Outline into the Outliner Window

Moving the Comments

Before going on, you'll probably want to make adjustments to the first bullet chart: its comments are crowding the title a bit and could stand to be a little lower on the page. The fastest way to get to the first page is to click directly on the page number you see at the lower left corner of the presentation window, and then to click on the number 1 in the list of presentation pages that appears. Now, click anywhere on the comments under the title. You'll see that all of the comments are a single object. Hold the mouse button down and drag them down the page a bit. ★

Adding Bullets with Bullet Chart Options

Say you'd like to transform the text points on the first or third page into bulleted points instead. Double-click on them. The Bullet Chart Options dialog box you'll see is an excellent specimen of the breed. Whenever you double-click on an object, its options, if it has any — and almost all objects do — will appear in a dialog box. Options are simply settings that affect the layout of that object. In a bar chart, for example, one option determines the degree to which the bars overlap one another. Another option determines whether a box you've drawn on a page has a three-dimensional effect (whether you see its sides along with its face).

One option in the Bullet Chart Options dialog box lets you add bullet points of various types to a group of comments. To make this happen, select Bullet from the list at the top of the dialog box. Then, at the control marked Font for Bullet, select ITC Zapf Dingbats. For these charts, use the small horizontal scroll bar within the dialog box to choose character number 34, a filled, five-pointed star—perfect for a Hollywood presentation. When you're satisfied with all the changes you've made in the dialog box, select OK, okay?

21

Adding a Data Chart

Now let's turn our attention to page 2: the chart that will show Harry's box-office projections. We've already decided we'll need a data chart to show these numbers, so turn to page 2 and then click on the words "Data Charts" in the Toolbox. When the Data Charts drawer opens, select the Column Chart tool (the first tool on the left) in order to begin a column chart. (A column chart is a bar chart with vertical bars.)

All of a sudden the Data Manager takes over the screen. That's what happens when you start any kind of data chart: Hollywood immediately pops open the Data Manager window so you can enter the data for the chart. If you've already got the figures in Lotus 1-2-3 or Excel, you can import them directly into the Data Manager. But in this case all you've got is a napkin where Harry scribbled some numbers, so you'll type them in directly.

Understanding the Data Manager

Take a look at the Data Manager window. Notice that it's made up of a large number of rectangular cells arranged in rows and columns. This is called a data *table*, and it's made for holding the numbers that will end up in a data *chart*. If you're familiar with a spreadsheet program like Lotus 1-2-3 or Excel, you'll recognize the data table's similarity to a spreadsheet. But, unlike a spreadsheet, a data table can't perform calculations on

numbers. It only holds them for charts.

Across the top, above eight of the data table's columns, you see numbered series headings: "Series 1," "Series 2," and so on. Each series heading stands for a different subject whose numeric story you want to tell. Don't worry that in this case we have only one story to tell — Harry's projections for *Lola's* box-office receipts. You can use as many vertical columns as you need, or as few. In this case all we'll fill in is Series 1.

In the first column, under "Labels," you'll type the list of regions Harry has isolated. When the final chart gets drawn, these labels will appear along the horizontal axis (the X-axis) of the chart.

Use the mouse or the keyboard's arrow keys to move the cursor to the cell with the letter "A" in it at the top of one of the columns. Next, click and drag the mouse to the right so that both columns A and B are highlighted. For our next trick, we'll increase the width of these two columns to make room for the labels and numbers they'll contain. Select Column Width on the Special menu and then type "1.5" (that's inches) next to where "Col. Width:" appears. Then, select OK.

Now, move the cursor down to the cell containing "Series 1" and type "Lola Box Office" right over the words "Series 1." Next move the cursor to the first empty cell in the

▼

The Data
Manager
appears
whenever you
start a data chart.

▼

A series is a
related set of
numbers.

▼

Labels are the
words that will
appear along the
chart's horizontal
axis (the X-axis).

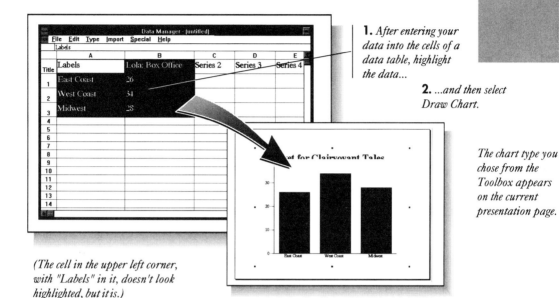

1. *After entering your data into the cells of a data table, highlight the data...*

2. *...and then select Draw Chart.*

The chart type you chose from the Toolbox appears on the current presentation page.

(The cell in the upper left corner, with "Labels" in it, doesn't look highlighted, but it is.)

Using Draw Chart to Generate a Data Chart from a Data Table

Labels column and type "East Coast" into it, "West Coast" into the cell below, and "Midwest" into the cell below that. Now you're ready to begin entering Harry's figures. Type these three figures below "Lola Box Office" in column A: 26, 34, 28. Your data table should now look like the one shown above.

To transform these numbers into a column chart, you simply highlight the data that you want to chart and then use the Draw Chart command on the File menu. Follow these steps: First, click on the cell with the word "Labels" inside. Next, hold the mouse button down while dragging to the right as far as column B and then down as far as the fourth cell; if you've gone just the right distance

you'll have highlighted the first four cells of both columns A and B — just the cells that hold your data and your labels. Now, select Draw Chart on the File menu. When Hollywood asks whether to "Save the current changes?" select No. (The data table is saved automatically with the chart. You'd only want to save it separately on disk if you thought you'd need it for another presentation, and that's doubtful here.)

Within a few seconds you'll see a column chart on the screen. It's not in the right position on the page, and it needs some design touches, but it's there and it's ready for your embellishments. You'll reposition it properly and give it a bit more pizzazz in a moment. ★

Changing a Data Chart's Options

Though the position of the new column chart is obviously amiss, there's nothing technically wrong with it — and it was certainly easy enough to create. But that's about all you can say positive about it. Your new column chart could do with a few design touches.

To make any changes to the chart — in fact, to make changes to any object you've placed on a Hollywood page — you must select the object first by clicking on it with the mouse. When eight small handles that look like little boxes surround it, you know the object is selected. With these handles, you can drag the edge or corner of the object to change its size and shape.

Use the handle in the upper right corner to resize the column chart: click on the handle and then drag it lower on the page so that the column

chart is neatly centered below the page title.

You've Got Other Options

Now let's give the chart a little Hollywood glamour by double-clicking on it to change its options. Column charts have six categories of options available on the large Column Chart dialog box that appears. You can see the full set of options within any of these categories by clicking on one of the six buttons that run down the left side of the dialog box. One category, Titles, lets you enter a main title, a legend title, and several other titles for the chart.

Going 3D

To snazz up the chart a bit, try the button labeled "3D Effect." On the 3D Effect dialog box that appears, click on the check box next to Turn on 3D and then select OK. Notice that the little miniature of the column

To select a chart, click on it once. To summon its options, double-click on it.

Data charts have several categories of options. When you double-click on a data chart, you'll see the categories as buttons in the dialog box.

Before Sliding Corner Handle Inward

After

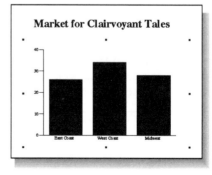

1. Double-clicking on the data chart produces the Column Chart dialog box.

Column Chart

Chart Style
Series
Titles
3D Effect
Axes
Tick Marks
Data Labels
Markers

To Data   OK   Cancel

3D Effect

Horizontal: 0.177 In.

Vertical: 0.150 In.

☒ Turn on 3D

OK   Cancel

2. Then, clicking on 3D Effect in the Column Chart dialog box produces this dialog box with 3D Effect options.

The column chart with 3D bars

Market for Clairvoyant Tales

3. Check this check box by clicking on it to turn on the 3D Effect for the column chart.

chart inside the dialog box now shows a column chart with some depth.

A Former Legend

Try another change. Click on the button labeled "Data Labels," select None under Legend Placement, and then select OK. Because you're displaying only a single subject in this chart (the projected box-office receipts of *Lola*), you don't need a legend to distinguish among several different sets of bars. If you had placed a legend on your data chart, it would now be gone.

Entitling

But now, without a legend, you do need a title for the chart, so click on the Titles group of options and then, into the Chart Title text box, type: "Projected Box Office Receipts."

Good. Now you've successfully modified the options for the chart. To see the result, select OK on the Column Chart options dialog box. You should see the effects of all the options changes you made on the revised chart that reappears on the screen.

Moving the Chart

At this point you may want to move the chart on the page a little more until you're satisfied with its appearance.

The principle you've learned here — double-clicking on an object to change its options — is central to the way Hollywood works. Nearly every object, whether it's a shape you draw with the Draw tools or a chart you create with the Data Charts or Text Charts tools, has options you can summon by double-clicking. ★

Putting a Design on the Master Page

The three pages of your presentation are already in pretty good shape. They tell your story clearly, and they're reasonably attractive, to boot. But you're working for Harry — showman *extraordinaire*. Why not make use of yet two more Hollywood tricks to make your presentation even better to look at!

With the tools available in the Toolbox drawer labeled "Draw," you can create graphic designs by drawing shapes on any page. But when you draw those shapes on the Master Page, they'll repeat on every page of your presentation. Let's try one such shape and see: a beveled box positioned just right so that each page title will seem to sit on a raised platform.

Positioning the Shape on a Presentation Page First

To be sure that your box will be positioned and sized correctly, it's best to create it first on one of the presentation pages, right where an actual page title sits. Then it can be moved to the same position on the Master Page.

Begin by turning to page 1, which has a good representative title. Now open the Draw drawer of the Toolbox by clicking on it once. The tools in this drawer let you create various shapes. Click on the first tool, though, the one with a picture of a box on it. Next, move the cursor to just above

and to the left of the page title. Click and hold the mouse button while moving the cursor to the right and then down just enough so that the box completely encloses the page title. Then release the mouse button. Your newly added box will completely obscure the page title. That's because Hollywood thinks you wanted to draw the box *on top* of the title. You'll fix that in a minute.

Now for the beveled edge. Any box can get a beveled edge. You simply change the box's options. Remember, to change an object's options you double-click on it. When you double-click on the box, you'll see a Rectangle Options dialog box with two controls: Chisel Effect and 3D Effect. You'll be using the Chisel Effect control.

Notice that the sample box shown under Chisel Effect is surrounded by small, round pushbuttons on all sides. Hollywood enhances the beveled-edge effect by making "light" seem to shine on the box. The pushbuttons determine the direction from which this pseudo light seems to come. Try "pushing" a few of the pushbuttons and you'll see.

For your box, let's have the light seem to come from the upper left. Click on the pushbutton on the upper left corner. Now you can use the scroll bar below the sample box to increase the size of the chiseled edge. Set the Amount of Chisel control to .10 inches.

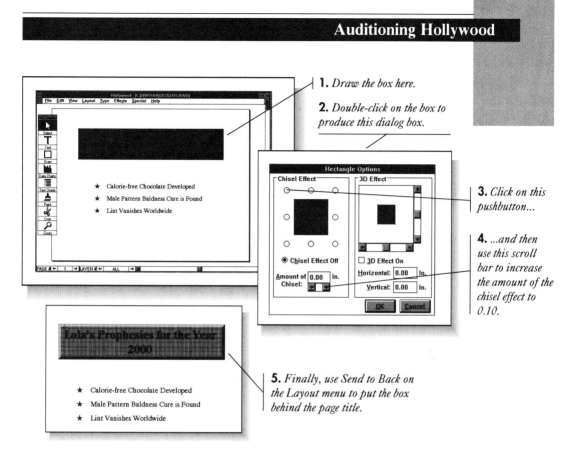

1. *Draw the box here.*

2. *Double-click on the box to produce this dialog box.*

3. *Click on this pushbutton...*

4. *...and then use this scroll bar to increase the amount of the chisel effect to 0.10.*

5. *Finally, use Send to Back on the Layout menu to put the box behind the page title.*

When you select OK to finish up, you'll see that the box you've drawn has a snazzy beveled edge. But it still obscures the page title! No problem. While the box is selected, use Send to Back on the Layout menu to send the box *behind* the page title. Now the page title appears properly atop the raised box.

Moving the Finished Box to the Master Page

To make the beveled box appear on every page, move it to the Master Page. First make sure the box is selected, and then select Cut on the Edit menu. This "cuts it out" and moves it to a temporary storage area.

Now turn to the Master Page by clicking on the page number at the bottom of the main presentation window and selecting Master from the list. Finally, select Paste from the Edit menu to paste the box into position. Go ahead and leaf through the pages of your presentation. You'll see the same snazzy box under the page title on every page.

The content of your presentation is complete. And you've even added a flourish with the beveled box. Now you can tinker with the presentation's overall design by modifying its color scheme or by applying a different template. You'll try each of these next. ★

Changing the Color Scheme

Every presentation has a special Hollywood device attached to it that designs the look of each object. This device is called a color scheme. The color scheme gives different types of objects specific designs. The color scheme sees, for example, that you're drawing an object with a Draw tool. It knows that every object drawn with a Draw tool gets a certain fill color. It also remembers that the desired typeface for each page title you create in the Outliner is a 24-point Swiss font in yellow, for example, and that each bullet in a bullet chart is bright red. The color scheme uses its rules to put the finishing design touches on each object as you create it.

A presentation starts with the color scheme listed in the preference file. But changing the color scheme attached to a presentation is very straightforward. As with most changes in Hollywood, you do it in a dialog box. To summon the Color Schemes dialog box, you select Color Schemes... on the Effects menu.

At first, the Color Schemes dialog box is small, showing only a single control for selecting one of the available color schemes. But you can expand it to show the rest of its controls by selecting More. Now, in the new and larger dialog box, you see quite a few more controls on the right. The two topmost controls, Chart Type and Chart Element, are particularly important.

The Chart Type control lets you select which object type to work on:

Bullet Chart, Data Charts, Main Page, Table Chart, or Tree Chart. And the Chart Element control lets you select which aspect of that object type you're setting up in the color scheme. When you select Bullet Chart as the chart type, you see these choices within the Chart Element control: Bullet Color, Sub-Title Type Style & Color, and Title Type Style & Color. You can create separate design rules (colors, fill patterns, and so on) for each chart element.

Try putting a color wash in the presentation's background. Select Main Page as the chart type and Page Background Color as the chart element. Now you can use the controls within the Color Schemes dialog box to select the attributes you want for the page background. In this case, click the button next to Color Wash to reveal a list of choices. Use the scroll bar next to the list to scroll to Black/Blue (the choices are arranged alphabetically) and then select it. The stunning Black/Blue color wash shows up immediately in the small preview of the page that you see.

Changing the Bullet Chart Titles Color

While fixing one problem, though, you've inadvertently created another. Because the bulleted text lines are now dark against a dark background, they're hard to read. You might want to change them to a brighter color, perhaps even white. Easy enough. Just select Bullet Chart as the chart

The color scheme helps you achieve uniformity in a presentation by applying the same design to all objects of the same type.

Of course, you can override the color scheme's control of an individual object, making unique design changes.

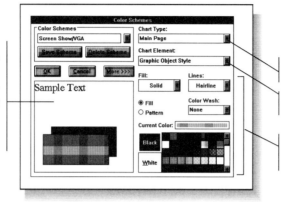

This sample chart previews the changes you make in the dialog box. Here, it shows the main page with text and graphic objects placed on top.

Click here to select a different chart type.

Click here to select a different chart element.

Use these controls to set up the chart element you've selected above.

type and Sub-Title Type Style & Color as the chart element. You'll see that the Current Color indicator shows black. Simply click on the white in the color palette, and the Current Color indicator is now white. So are the sub-titles in the dialog box's miniature.

Uh-oh. The title of the bullet chart looks even *worse* against its background. It's black against a nearly black background. But remember: your titles are going to appear on top of a beveled box. What we'll do next is select a light color to fill the beveled box, creating a contrast with the black titles.

Changing Beveled Box Color

The beveled box is a graphic object placed directly on the background page. Its design rules are stored in the color scheme under the Main Page chart type and the Graphic Object Style chart element. So if you change the design rules for Graphic Object Style, you'll be changing the design of every graphic object you place directly on the background page

(boxes, lines, circles, curves, and other shapes). That's no problem here because the beveled box is the only graphic object you plan to add to the presentation. If you add more, though, you can always override the color scheme's design choices for those new objects individually.

To put a suitable color inside the box, select Main Page with the Chart Type control and Graphic Object Style with the Chart Element control. Then, use the scroll bar next to the color palette to scroll to the very lightest yellow and click on it.

Now, let's save this new color scheme with its own name so that you can use it again on another presentation. At the upper left corner of the dialog box, in the Color Schemes text box, highlight the words "Screen Show/VGA" and then type "Lola" in their place.

You've now replaced the original color scheme name with your own. Select Save Scheme to save the revised color scheme, and select OK to view the changes you've made to the presentation. ★

Using Presentation View and Spell Checking

Up to now, you've worked either with the outline (seeing the text for your entire presentation but none of the graphics) or on individual pages. But wouldn't it be nice to see all the pages simultaneously — or at least a good sampling — so you could check for consistency and make sure their order is correct? Hollywood provides that capability in its Presentation View.

While the Outliner window shows you the text content of the presentation, and the main presentation window shows you the design of a single page, Presentation View shows you nine miniature presentation pages all in one window. These miniatures are referred to as "thumbnails." You can't change the contents of individual pages while in Presentation View, nor can you change their design, but you can change their order, delete pages that you no longer want, and copy pages from one place in the presentation to another.

Copying a page can come in handy if you have a page design you like very much and wish to repeat on another page. Once you've copied it in Presentation View, you can go to the copy and change its text content: new information, same design. Presentation View is also handy for navigating from one part of the presentation to another. In Presentation View, you can quickly find the page you want to work on and then

double-click on it. The page appears full screen in the main presentation window.

Getting to Presentation View

To look at your work in Presentation View, select Presentation... on the View menu. In a moment, you'll see nine thumbnail versions of your pages. You can imagine that these are actually 35mm slides laid out on a light table that illuminates them from below. A light table makes it easy to shuffle 35mm slides around until you find the order you like. Presentation View lets you do the same thing by simply dragging the miniatures on the screen from one position to another.

Assume for the moment that you need to switch the second and third pages of your presentation: Harry says he wants to address the lucrative movie tie-ins before delivering his market projections for the film. That's easily done. Simply click and hold the mouse button down on the third page and slide it to position No. 2. The page that was in the second position jumps ahead to the third position. If you were to return to the presentation outline now, you'd see that the order of the main topics has been rearranged also.

Try double-clicking on the miniature of the column chart, which is now the third page in the presentation. In a moment you'll see the page full screen and, sure enough,

---

▼

Presentation View gives you a long shot of nine of your presentation pages at a time.

▼

You can copy a page in Presentation View to duplicate a design.

▼

Double-clicking on a thumbnail takes you right to that page in the main Hollywood window.

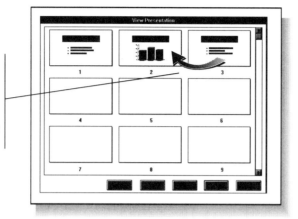

In Presentation View, you can drag a page to a new position in the presentation. The rest of the pages will readjust.

Or, you can double-click on any page to go right to that page.

The Presentation View Window

the page indicator at the lower left corner shows that this is now page 3.

Spell Checking

Your presentation is brief, so you haven't had much chance to make one of those killer typographical errors that leave your audience giggling and snorting. To be sure they never get that chance, you'll want to use Hollywood's built-in spell checker.

Like any spell checker, it looks for words not in its dictionary. When it finds one, it points out the unfamiliar word and offers a few alternate spellings from which to choose.

You can spell check an individual page while working in the main presentation window, but it's best to spell check an entire presentation at once, which you can do in the Outliner window.

To return to the Outliner, select the Bullet Chart tool from the Text Charts drawer of the Toolbox once again.

If you find that some of the text seems to be missing from the outline, it may just be that it's invisible against the Outliner window's background, which displays the color scheme's color choices. You may want to press F6 to call up the color palette and then select an alternate color for the background, perhaps gray, by clicking on gray in the color palette. Then select Fill and click on OK.

Now, select Check Spelling... from the Special menu and then select Start on the next dialog box. The spell checker finds the first unfamiliar word and displays it with a list of alternate suggestions. You can highlight a suggestion and then select Change to replace the word, or you can Ignore the word if you know it is correct, such as the name "Lola."

When the spelling check is finished, Hollywood pops up a "Spelling Check Completed!" message. Now it's time to save all your work. ★

Saving Your Work

▼

Templates can automatically format a presentation top to bottom.

▼

Hollywood comes with templates suited for several common output devices, and you can create your own, too.

Y our presentation is complete. You've created a stunning set of pages that Harry surely will be proud to show. Now you should save your work on disk.

Hollywood saves an entire presentation in a single file. This keeps all of the charts together in one place, making it easy to move them from one computer to another. Binding all the pages in a single unit is also what makes it possible to quickly change the color scheme that affects them all, or to add a graphic to every page simply by placing it on the Master Page.

To save a presentation, simply select Save on the File menu and then type in a standard DOS filename of up to eight characters. (The cursor is already in the Filename text box on the Save Presentation As dialog box.) Hollywood automatically appends the three-letter extension .HWD to the filename.

You'll see two buttons at the lower left of the dialog box. Save As Presentation is automatically selected. If you select Save As Template instead, Hollywood saves the presentation as a file that you can use to format another presentation in the future. In that case, Hollywood appends an .HWT extension to the template filename.

Saving a Presentation as a Template

A template is one of Hollywood's most powerful devices. Simply put,

it's a presentation that's been saved as a model for other presentations. Once a presentation is finished, you can apply a template to it to give it the same formatting you used successfully in an earlier presentation. The template changes your presentation's color scheme, it copies the items on its own Master Page onto your new one, and it repositions your charts so that they occupy the same position on the page as they did in the template presentation.

Hollywood comes with several professionally designed templates geared for different output devices. A few templates are designed for a black-and-white laser printer, for example. A few more are designed for 35mm color slides. By using a template, you can format a presentation from top to bottom with a single menu selection.

Examining Hollywood's Built-in Templates

You won't actually be employing any templates during this brief Hollywood tour, but if you'd like to see how the templates that come with Hollywood look, you can do so by selecting Get Template... from the Special menu. Next, select the Template directory using the Directories control. You should now see a list of files with .HWT extensions. Click *once* on any of these files and select Show Sample on the Get Template dialog box. Now you

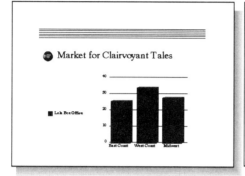

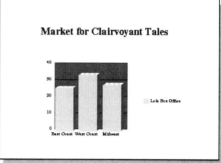

*The Same Presentation
Page Formatted by Four
Different Templates*

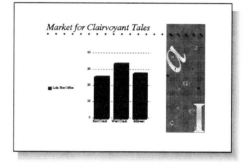

can use the scroll bar just to the right of the sample to move through that template and see its various page designs.

Were you actually to put the template to work, Hollywood would automatically find the page design in the template that most closely matches each page of your presentation, and it would apply the template's design to your page. Should it find two or more template pages that match the layout of your page (two pages that have, for example, a page title and a single data chart), it would pop open a window and let you choose which design to use.

When you've finished examining Hollywood's built-in templates, select Cancel to close up the Get Templates dialog box so you can go on and take a look at a few more of Hollywood's special features. ★

A Few Brief Detours

Y ou've used enough of Hollywood's capabilities to create a truly attractive presentation, but you still haven't seen all the tricks up Hollywood's sleeve. Let's take a quick peek at a few more parts of the program.

The Chart Gallery

When you're ready to start a data chart, instead of working with one of the data chart tools from the Toolbox,

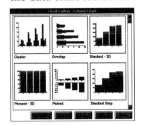

as we did, you can select Chart Gallery on the Special menu. The Chart Gallery holds a number of prefabricated designs for each chart type. By browsing through the Chart Gallery, you can select a chart that's ready to go rather than start from scratch.

Take a walk into the Chart Gallery by selecting Chart Gallery on the Special menu. At first, all you see are six column chart designs. But as you use the scroll bar at the right to browse through the rest of the gallery, you'll see a few designs for each different data chart type. Each design is actually a different combination of chart options. You can use any of these designs any time you need to create a data chart. In fact, you can even save your own custom-made charts in the Chart Gallery

simply by copying a finished data chart into it.

The Graphic Library

The Graphic Library holds professionally drawn pictures that can be incorporated into a presentation.

You can pull any of these pictures onto a single presentation page, or make it appear on every page by placing it on the Master Page. You can also deposit graphics you've drawn yourself into the Library and then "check them out" again anytime in the future. Some kinds of graphics you might want to store are logos you've drawn or images you've scanned. Perhaps your team's mascot should have its own place in the Graphic Library.

Screen Shows

A Hollywood screen show is an animated presentation of your pages shown right on the computer screen. A screen show can be an excellent alternative to the standard 35mm slide presentation or overhead "foil" presentation, particularly if you've got a video projector that can project a computer display or if you can gather a small group around a large computer screen. Screen shows offer something slide shows simply cannot: animation.

The Chart Gallery holds data chart designs. You can use any of its designs when you start a new data chart.

The Graphic Library holds clip art images you can use to dress up your presentation pages. You can store your own graphics there, too.

Screen shows offer an array of dazzling effects for making the transitions from one presentation page to the next: fading to black and then fading in on a new page, perhaps, or having the new page wipe onto the screen from the side.

You also can create charts that automatically reveal themselves one step at a time during the course of a screen show. These are called progressive builds, and they're an effective way to add a little drama to a presentation. You can even create *illustrations* that appear gradually, one piece at a time, by drawing each piece on a different "layer." Layers are like transparent overlays that you can lay down one upon another, slowly building an image. In a screen show you can reveal the image one layer at a time, and even use fancy transition effects to do so. ★

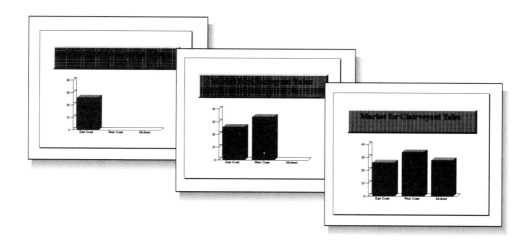

Screen shows can progressively build data and text charts. Here, the column chart in the Lola *presentation is built bar by bar. Each bar will fade into view as Harry talks about it.*

And You Haven't Even Seen...

By now you must think you've seen it all. Not by a long shot. You haven't even seen Hollywood's two other chart types: table charts and tree charts. They're not as common as bullet charts and data charts, but they serve very important functions nonetheless.

Table charts are tables of data, usually text but sometimes numbers, that you can format and position on any presentation page. They're really data tables from the Data Manager that you've prettied up a bit and had Hollywood reproduce on a page.

Tree charts are often called organization charts. They usually diagram the pyramid structure of an organization, although you can flip them on their side and make them into flow charts.

Both table and tree charts are considered text charts, so you'll find tools to create them with in the Text Charts drawer of the Toolbox, next to the Bullet Chart tool. Table and tree charts are also like data charts, though, in that you add them to presentation pages you've already created. They stick to those pages even if the pages are moved around in the Outliner or in Presentation View.

When you select the Table Chart tool to start a table chart, Hollywood opens the Data Manager window so that you can create the data table for the chart. When you select the Tree Chart tool to start a tree chart, Hollywood opens the Outliner window instead. The branch structure of the mini-outline you create becomes the branch structure of the tree.

So, bullet charts and tree charts get their start in the Outliner, and data charts and table charts get their start in the Data Manager. A good way of thinking about Hollywood's organization is this: The Outliner and Data Manager are where you work with the *content* of a chart. The main presentation window is where you work with its *appearance*.

Generating Handouts and Speaker's Notes

Once you've created a presentation, you can ask Hollywood to produce two useful additions to the main series of pages. A single handout page can show up to six of your presentation pages, reduced to fit on the page. With a handout page, your audience walks away from your presentation with a copy for fond recall later.

A notes page gives the speaker at the podium a miniature of each presentation page, including a blank area below in which he can write or type his notes.

Hollywood's Deluxe Image-Editing Tools

Not only can Hollywood draw a wide variety of shapes on a page, but it can make changes to them in ways usually seen only in advanced

---

▼

The Data Charts and Text Charts drawers of the Toolbox hold many other chart styles.

▼

Creating handouts and speaker's notes is automatic in Hollywood.

▼

Hollywood's unique drawing features rival those found in high-end illustration software.

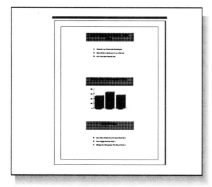

A Handout Page Showing Several Presentation Pages

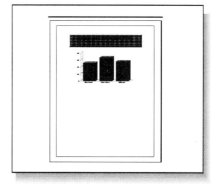

A Notes Page Showing Space Below Image for Speaker's Notes

illustration software programs. You can duplicate an object, for example, making as many copies as you wish across the page, their tints gradually progressing from one hue to another. You can move objects in front of or behind other objects. You can even align objects automatically with other objects or with designated spots on the page.

Hollywood provides still more editing tools. After you've drawn a polygon, you can use Polygon Edit to move each of its corners. After you've

drawn a text object, you can rotate it, curve it, shadow it, or even reverse the image, flipping it upside down or from right to left.

There's still much more, but seeing it all will be far more instructive than hearing about it. So dig in to the chapters that follow. One by one, you'll learn about each of Hollywood's amazing powers. Taken all together, they're simply the best presentation-making package you can get. ★

Where To from Here?

Next: Outlining the Presentation
Adding Bullet and Data
  Charts
Adding Other Chart Types
Adding the Trimmings: Extra
  Text and Graphics
Formatting the Presentation
Showing Off Your Work

Now it's time to begin taking a look at each step in assembling a Hollywood presentation one by one. You'll begin by trying out Hollywood's Outliner, where you enter the sequence of a presentation. Before you're through with the next chapter, you'll already have all the pages of your presentation.

The SCREENPLAY

Outlining a Presentation

In This Chapter

———◆———

What Is the Outliner?

Hollywood offers two very different ways to put together a presentation. In the first, you create the entire presentation on the fly, putting together its pages one by one. In the second, you work out an outline for the presentation first, and then spawn all of the presentation pages from it. This second method is the focus of this chapter for several reasons.

First, a presentation can hardly help but benefit from the forethought you put into it as you work on its outline. But just as important, the Outliner, which is where you create and organize outlines, is absolutely central to Hollywood. The presentation outline determines the order of the presentation pages and it's also the source for bullet charts, the most widely used type of presentation chart. Nearly every presentation has at least one bullet chart, and many presentations have nothing else but bullet charts.

An Overview of the Outliner

The Outliner comes out from behind the scenes whenever you call for it, usually when you start organizing a presentation. It appears on the screen in its own window, one you can move or resize as you would any other window. The outline you enter into the Outliner looks just like any conventional outline, with main topics, subtopics, and sub-subtopics, all arranged in an indented list.

Each main topic you enter into the outline becomes the title of a new

page when you use the Draw Chart command. The comments you've typed in below the main topics appear on the presentation pages just below the page titles. After the comments are on the pages, you can put bullets in front of the comments to create bullet points. That's all there is to creating a series of bullet charts. You enter into the Outliner a list of topics with several comments below each and then use Draw Chart.

Before you use Draw Chart, though, you may want to rework the outline, reorganizing its topics or adding additional subtopics for more detail. Later in this chapter, you'll learn how. You'll also learn how to print the finished outline so you'll have a paper copy at hand for easy reference.

After you've roughed out the basic outline, you may see that some of its topics are stories that are best told with numbers rather than with words. These stories you'll want to relate with data charts rather than with text charts. Other stories might be better

▼

A presentation's bullet charts come from its outline.

▼

Main topics in the outline become page titles. The indented items underneath become bulleted text points.

▼

At first, enter the messages you want to get across about each main topic. Later, you can delete those that you'll replace with graphic charts.

40

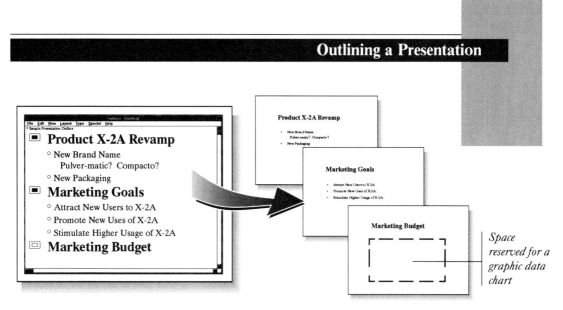

Space reserved for a graphic data chart

Using Draw Chart to Generate Presentation Pages from an Outline

told with organization charts that can depict a structure, or table charts that have side-by-side columns of text or numbers. To make space for these charts under the page titles, you won't enter subtopics under these main topics or you'll delete any comments you've already entered (you've got them on a printed copy of the outline should you forget the points you want to make in a data table or tree chart). Later, after you've used Draw Chart, you'll add each of these charts to the presentation pages.

Two Paths to a Presentation

Creating an outline is not the only way to build a presentation. The other approach is to create a presentation's pages one by one, finishing one page and then starting the next. With this method, you use the Text tool to manually place lines of text on some pages, the Text Charts tool to place table and tree charts on other pages, and the Data Charts tool to construct graphic charts on still other pages. But even if you follow this approach, Hollywood surreptitiously builds an outline of your work behind the scenes. It's as though Hollywood knows that sooner or later you'll want to use the outline to rearrange the presentation's order, add new topics, and delete others.

Next, you'll learn how to create an outline and start a presentation. ★

Three Easy Steps to a Presentation Outline

1. Click on the Bullet Chart tool to open the Outliner.
2. Enter a list of page titles with text points indented under each.
3. Use Draw Chart to convert the outline into presentation pages.

Creating the Presentation Outline

Use the Bullet Chart tool in the Text Charts drawer to get to the Outliner.

The same indented pattern of text you enter under a topic in the presentation outline appears on a page under the page title.

Refer to the chapter on working with text to learn special ways to format the text in the Outliner.

T o start the main presentation outline, open the Text Charts drawer of the Toolbox and select the Bullet Chart tool. Why use the Bullet Chart tool to get to the Outliner? Because an outline becomes a series of bullet charts. In fact, you can think of it *as* a series of bullet charts. Hollywood creates them when you use Draw Chart.

When the Outliner window appears, you'll see a small dot in its upper left corner and, below that, a double rectangle followed by a large, flashing typing cursor.

You can enter a title for the outline next to the small dot. The outline title appears in the Outliner window, but not in the presentation.

Start entering the list of topics you plan to cover by moving the cursor back down next to the double rectangle. Type a few words that summarize the topic, and then press Enter to move down a line. Now, either type a second main topic (you're already in position to do that) or prepare to type comments about the first topic by pressing Tab. This moves the cursor to the right one step. (With a mouse, you can click and hold on the line marker, a circle at the beginning of the line, and drag to the right.) Type each comment on a separate line, and then, after you've entered all comments, press Enter to move down one more line. To get back to the left to the level of the main topics, press Shift-Tab or drag the next line marker to the left with the mouse. Continue this process until you've exhausted the entire list of topics you want to present.

You'll notice that when a topic has comments underneath it, the line marker at the left is filled rather than hollow. You'll also find that rectangular markers indicate presentation pages that already exist; circles indicate pages yet to be made.

Details, Details

To add further detail to any of the comments in the outline, move the cursor to the end of the comment and then press Enter to open a new line below. Then start a third-level entry by pressing Tab or dragging the line marker over to the right another level. You can continue adding detail at deeper and deeper levels in the outline, creating a heavily indented outline structure. The exact same outline structure will show up on the presentation page later.

Seeing More or Less

To temporarily hide comments that are indented under a main topic, double-click on the marker in front of the topic. This is called collapsing a part of the outline; it lets you temporarily ignore some of the detail you've entered. You can collapse entries under any of the markers at any level in the outline. Double-clicking again on a marker expands all the collapsed comments below it.

Enter an outline title here.

Line marker

Press Tab to indent to the comment level.

Press Shift-Tab to get back up to the main topic level.

Outliner [Untitled]

File Edit View Layout Type Special Help

• Presentation Outline Title

■ **Main Topic 1**
    • Comment 1
      ○ Detail 1
      ○ Detail 2
      ○ Comment 2

■ **Main Topic 2**
    • Comment 1
      ○ Detail 1
      ○ Detail 2

▭ **Main Topic 3**

Main topics become page titles.

Comments and Detail items become text under page titles.

An outline in the Outliner window

Make Room for Data

Undoubtedly, some of the comments you've entered into the outline describe numeric information, such as rising profits or falling costs. Perhaps you'll decide these subjects are better told with data charts than with words. By simply deleting the comments under a particular main topic, you'll be leaving clear the space under one of the page titles. In the next two chapters, you'll learn how to fill that space with a data, table, or tree chart.

To delete one of the comments, click on the circle preceding the comment, and then press Del (Delete) on the keyboard.

The Last Steps

If you'd like to reorganize the outline or add topics you omitted earlier, now is the time to do it. Actually, any time is the time to rearrange the outline. You can do so even after you've added all the data, table, and tree charts you need to complete the presentation. But if you want to make no more changes to the outline, you can use Draw Chart on the File menu to leave the Outliner and have Hollywood generate presentation pages from the presentation outline. You'll read about Draw Chart a little later in this chapter. ★

Why Is Text in the Outliner So Big?

Don't be surprised if the text in the Outliner looks centered or very large. All Hollywood is doing is letting you see how it will look in the finished bullet charts. You can reduce the text size and left-align it while you work in the Outliner by selecting the text and using the Type menu commands. Chapter 7 covers this. To let the color scheme take control once again before you use Draw Chart, select Use Color Scheme on the Layout menu.

Reorganizing an Outline

Change the order of topics in the outline to change the order of pages in the presentation.

Clicking on a line marker selects that line and all of its subordinate entries.

You can move around whole sections of an outline and copy them to other outlines, too.

You certainly have a right to change your mind, and Hollywood even makes it easy. It lets you go back and rearrange the outline structure of a presentation anytime you want, even after you've used Draw Chart to create the presentation pages. Returning to the Outliner from Hollywood's view of individual pages is discussed on the following two pages. Changing the outline while you're in the Outliner is covered here.

Moving, Promoting, and Demoting Entries

Changing the order of topics as you're developing the outline is probably what you'll do the most. But just as easy is promoting indented comments up to first-level topics so they get their own presentation pages, or demoting topics so they become comments on the pages of other topics.

The key to manipulating an entry in an outline is to click once on the marker at its left. This selects the item plus any indented comments below; what you've selected is indicated by a dashed box around the whole group. From there, you can perform a whole variety of actions on the part of the outline you've selected. For example, you can move it by simply dragging its marker to a new position in the outline. Move Up and Move Down on the Layout menu give you keyboard alternatives.

As you drag with the mouse, you won't see the area of the outline you've selected move. Instead, a small triangular marker moves through the outline, pointing to where the text will appear when you release the mouse. You can drag a portion of the outline anywhere else in the outline and to any indented level.

Cutting and Pasting Entries

After you've selected an entry and its subordinates in the outline, you can also use Cut or Copy on the Edit menu to move it to the Windows Clipboard. (Using Clear — or pressing the Del key — deletes for good whatever is selected.)

The Windows Clipboard temporarily holds whatever you cut or copy from any Windows application. In this case, it holds text from an outline that you've cut or copied. You can bring the Clipboard contents into another outline by opening the other outline (with Open on the Outliner's File menu) and then choosing Paste on the Outliner's Edit menu. When the second outline opens, the first one closes. The Outliner can handle only one outline at a time.

Cut, Copy, Clear, and Paste can also be used to move a portion of a line — perhaps just a few words — from one entry to another within an outline. To do that you highlight only those words with the mouse or the keyboard and then use one of the "C" commands.

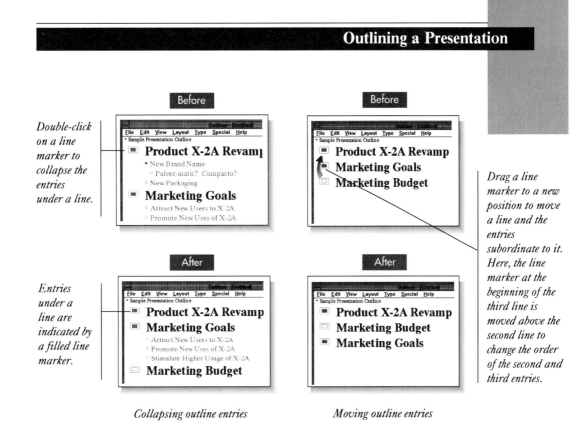

Double-click on a line marker to collapse the entries under a line.

Entries under a line are indicated by a filled line marker.

Drag a line marker to a new position to move a line and the entries subordinate to it. Here, the line marker at the beginning of the third line is moved above the second line to change the order of the second and third entries.

Collapsing outline entries

Moving outline entries

Formatting Text in the Outline

The color scheme settings that determine the type style and type size for bullet charts also control all the type created in the Outliner. Main topics get one type style, and the rest of the text gets another—both in the outline and in bullet charts. That helps you see while working in the Outliner how the text will look in your bullet charts.

But you can also highlight any text in the Outliner and then use the commands on the Type menu to change how certain words or lines of text will look in a bullet chart. (You can always revert back to the color scheme's text styles by selecting Use Color Scheme on the Outliner's Layout menu.)

To highlight individual words in an outline, wipe across them with the mouse while the mouse button is pressed or hold the Shift key as you move the cursor across them with the arrow keys. Then, select a character attribute on the Type menu, such as Bold, Italic, or Underline. To change the typeface of text, you can use Font and Size on the Type menu, or you can use Styles, also on the Type menu, to select a predefined combination of settings. You'll learn all about formatting text and setting up styles in Chapter 6. To print an outline you've created, use Print on the menu or press Ctrl-P. ★

From Outline to Pages and Back

B y now, your outline is complete. You've confirmed the topics you'll present and the sequence they'll follow. You've also revised the comments below the topics so that they're sharp, clear statements, and you've deleted those comments that tell stories you'll communicate with data, table, or organization charts. Now comes the time to convert the outline into the pages of a presentation. Draw Chart on the Outliner's File menu does this.

When you use Draw Chart, Hollywood asks whether to save the outline as a file (outline files get an .OUT extension). Saving the outline lets you use it as part of a larger presentation that you'll prepare later. If the outline covers only one aspect of your business, you can create a master presentation by combining this outline with other saved outlines, copying and pasting them into an all-inclusive outline.

To save an outline as a file, use Save on the Outliner's File menu or press Ctrl-S, and then type a filename where requested in the Save Outline As dialog box.

From Outline to Pages

Whether or not you save an outline for future use, you'll see one of your presentation pages full screen as soon as you use Draw Chart. Which one you see is determined by where in the outline the cursor was when you used Draw Chart. If the cursor was somewhere on the first topic in the outline, you'll see the first page. If the cursor was on the last topic, you'll see the last page, and so on. Keep this in mind should you revise the outline later; having the cursor somewhere on the revised topic when you again use Draw Chart will give you an immediate look at your revised presentation page.

▼

The Draw Chart command creates all of the presentation pages from the outline.

▼

Save an outline as a file on disk to use again later, perhaps as part of a larger presentation.

▼

Selecting the Bullet Chart tool while working on a presentation page opens the Outliner again. You can only edit page titles and the text of bullet charts within the Outliner.

★ Importing an Outline

If you've already got an outline for a presentation in your word processor, you can easily import it into Hollywood's Outliner, saving you the work of typing it all over again. Just make sure the outline's indented levels were created using either tabs or spaces. Then, save it as an ASCII text file. In Hollywood's Outliner, use Import Text on the File menu and select the ASCII file you just saved. Hollywood asks whether the ASCII file contains numbered items (i.e., whether the lines in the outline are numbered). If it does and you select Yes, Hollywood removes the numbers automatically so they don't appear on the final charts. You'll see the outline appear in the Outliner, just as if you'd typed it in.

Browsing Your Pages

At the very bottom of the presentation window, you'll see the current page number, flanked on the left and right by arrows. You can click on these arrows to turn the pages of the presentation. Click on the current page number instead, and you'll see a list of page numbers you can click on to jump to a specific page.

As you move through the presentation, you'll see that the topics you entered into the outline have indeed become the titles of the pages, and that the comments have become indented lists below the titles. Just as promised.

Back to the Outline

Even after you've created the actual presentation pages from the outline, you can return to the outline at any time to change the presentation's structure or revise some of the text in its text charts. To return to the outline, click on the Bullet Chart tool still visible in the Toolbox. This reopens the Outliner window where you'll see the main presentation outline. Another way back to the outline is with the Text tool: just click with it on any of the text on the page and then either press Ctrl-D or use Data Table/Outline on the View menu. This second method, highlighting text, conveniently returns you to that very text in the Outliner. You may prefer to use it to quickly get to the text you want to change.

Back in the Outliner, you can make changes to the outline and then use Draw Chart to update the presentation. If you've saved the outline in a file, Hollywood asks whether to save the current changes you've made. Select Yes to update the saved file or No if for some reason you'd want to update the presentation but leave the saved version of the outline as is. ★

Where To from Here?

Now that you've outlined the presentation's structure and generated its pages from the outline, you're ready to transform the text charts you already have into bullet charts, and add data charts and other chart types to the presentation. That's up next.

The LEADING ROLES

Adding Bullet Charts and Data Charts

In This Chapter

◆

What is a Bullet Chart?

These days, newspapers and magazines are chock full of colorful charts and graphs, and yet presentation slides still deliver mostly text. By some estimates, over 80 percent of the presentations given every day are filled with nothing but text.

You'll probably be making lots of text charts, too — which is why this chapter gives them top billing. Later in the chapter you'll learn about graphic charts as well, but clearly text comes first. And the most important text chart of all is the bullet chart.

Bullet charts are a direct offshoot of the work you've already done in the Outliner. What's more, they're straightforward and simple to modify, so they're a good place to cut your teeth on some of Hollywood's basic principles. You'll learn, for example, the difference between Hollywood's menu commands and its chart options. You'll also learn how to work with Hollywood objects. Don't worry if these concepts sound foreign. They'll become familiar soon enough.

Getting the Point

Anyone who's ever seen a chalk-talk has seen a speaker put text charts to use — introducing an agenda and capsulizing key points as each is made. Good speakers know that a statement that's seen as well as heard has a more powerful and longer-lasting impact. The text

charts you make in Hollywood are called *bullet charts*, even when they don't have true bullet shapes at the beginning of each line, as you'd expect.

Usually, bullet charts have a title at the top and a list of statements below. Think back to the previous chapter and you'll recognize these as the main topics and indented comments you've entered into the presentation outline. If it helps, you can picture a series of bullet charts as nothing more than the presentation outline chopped up and spread out among a series of pages. Each page displays one main topic from the outline and all of the indented text that was below it.

This way of picturing the relationship between bullet charts and the outline isn't as frivolous as it sounds. You'll soon see that to change the content of a bullet chart, you must return to the outline and make it there. Even if you *try* to change a bullet chart directly, Hollywood will pop open the Outliner window and force you to make your change on the outline instead.

Bullet Chart Objects

After you've created a presentation outline and used Draw Chart to convert it to pages, you'll find that each bullet chart is actually composed of two objects: the title is one, and the text lines below it are a second. When you click on the title, handles appear at the sides and corners of an imaginary

---

▼

Bullet charts are really the main topics and indented comments you entered into the outline.

▼

You can change the content of bullet charts only in the Outliner.

Today's Agenda

- Introductions and Backslapping
- Announcements
- Old Business
- Report to the Committee
- New Business
- Cocktails

Our Five Step Plan

1. Investigate alternatives
2. Cost/benefit analysis
3. Prepare recommendations
4. Implement decision
5. Evaluate results

Some Sample Bullet Charts

frame that surrounds it. But when you click on one of the text comments instead, handles mark a frame that surrounds the entire group of comments, showing you that they're all one object.

As with any object in Hollywood, you can drag either the title or the group of comments to a new position simply by clicking on it anywhere, holding the mouse button down, and then dragging. You also can drag the side handles of either object out from the center so that the text inside the frame spreads out across the page and doesn't wrap to a new line so quickly. Think of it as widening the margins.

Formatting the Chart

It's a Hollywood axiom that you can change the appearance of an object

two ways: by clicking on it once to select it, then using menu commands to change its format; or by double-clicking on it to bring forth a dialog box, then changing the options that the box presents. Each method provides control over different aspects of an object's appearance.

One key difference between menu commands and options is this: Menus are where you go to make the kind of changes that might be made to any or all objects, such as changing their color. An options dialog box is where you go if the change you want to make could only apply to the kind of object you're working on, such as choosing the style of bullet.

Using menu commands and bullet chart options is the next subject. ★

Four Easy Steps to a Bullet Chart

Creating a series of bullet charts takes but a few easy steps:
1. Typing topics with indented comments below into an outline.
2. Using Draw Chart to generate pages with bullet charts on them.
3. Returning to the outline to make any needed changes to the text, then using Draw Chart again.
4. Repositioning the title or comments object with the mouse, if necessary.

Changing the Look of a Bullet Chart

B y selecting (clicking on) one of the objects in a bullet chart — title or comments — you can then use any of the Type menu commands to change the formatting of its characters: Bold, Italic, and Underline do just what you'd think. Or you can use Styles on the Type menu to select a previously established *combination* of Type menu settings. (You'll learn all about setting up and using styles in Chapter 6.)

The colors command on the Effects menu is also available to you when you're formatting bullet charts. You can use it to change the color of either the title or comments of your bullet chart. Once you've selected which object to change, press F6 or choose Colors on the Effects menu. Then click on a color in the Color Palette window. Be sure, though, that you click on the color palette's Text pushbutton when you select the color.

Loading a Chart with Bullets

Double-clicking on any object in a bullet chart summons the Bullet Chart Options dialog box. Among the many controls you'll find here are ones that add bullets — all kinds of bullets — in front of your text points.

The pushbuttons in the upper portion of the dialog box will automatically number or letter your points. Or you can choose a graphic symbol to serve as the bullets in front of each comment line. The sample

box on the right demonstrates the result of each option.

If you decide to use graphic bullets, click on the Bullets pushbutton, and then use the scroll bar below to scroll through the available bullet shapes. If you're not happy with the shapes you see, choose a different font by clicking on Font for Bullet. For example, if you've selected Dutch 801 Bold, you can use the scroll bar to choose bullet symbol No. 361, a happy face. You're likely to find the best bullets after you select the ITC Zapf Dingbats font.

If you choose the pushbutton labeled Active Bullet, you'll get a bullet that shows up only in a screen show, as part of a progressive build. Both screen shows and progressive builds are covered later, in Chapter 9.

After selecting all the options you want, select OK on the Bullet Chart Options dialog box. Your changes will take effect immediately, and you'll see bullets appear in front of the text you'd selected.

Now bullet charts are a single exception in Hollywood to the rule that options always apply only to a single object. In the case of bullet charts — and only with bullet charts — when you put bullets in front of one set of comments, the same bullets appear in front of the comments in every bullet chart in your presentation. On one hand, it's a convenience, but on the other hand, it's inflexible. You can't turn off or

---

▼

You can use the Type menu and Color on the Effects menu to format bullet charts.

▼

Bullet charts are an exception to the rule that options affect only one chart: Turn on bullets for one bullet chart and the same bullets appear on all bullet charts.

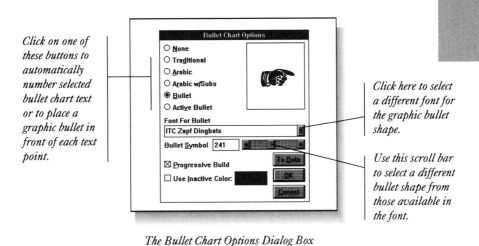

Click on one of these buttons to automatically number selected bullet chart text or to place a graphic bullet in front of each text point.

Click here to select a different font for the graphic bullet shape.

Use this scroll bar to select a different bullet shape from those available in the font.

The Bullet Chart Options Dialog Box

change the bullets for a single bullet chart. If you try, the same thing happens on all the bullet charts.

The Progressive Build and Use Inactive Color options are for building bullet charts line by line in screen shows. You'll learn about these options in Chapter 9.

How the Color Scheme is Involved

When you first view a set of bullet charts fresh from the outline, you'll notice that each chart has the same text color and text size and that the bullets are all the same color. These starting attributes are controlled by whatever color scheme is attached to the presentation. The color scheme holds a default style for chart titles, another for comments (called "subtitles" by the color scheme), plus a default color for the graphic bullets. Change these settings in the color scheme and you can change the look of all bullet charts simultaneously. By selecting individual bullet chart objects, you can then override the color scheme's settings by choosing different Type menu settings and different colors for individual charts. ★

Creating Special Styles for Bullet Charts

As you work with Hollywood, you'll find that it always puts the same amount of space between lines of bulleted text. That distance may be fine when you've got six or eight bulleted points on a page, but when you've got only two or three, you'd like a way to spread them out. There is a way to do it. It's possible to create a special style — one with additional space between lines — for use when a bullet chart has only a few lines. You'll find the details in Chapter 6.

What Is a Data Chart?

Y ou're certainly familiar with data charts—bar charts, pie charts, line charts, and others. You see them all over the place. Everyone knows how stylishly they relate stories about numbers. But for all their glamour, in Hollywood they're just like any other object in a presentation, subject to the very same rules and regulations.

A data chart is really just another object. It follows all of the same rules as objects.

Drawing a Data Chart

You create a data chart by using one of the data chart tools in the Toolbox. You place it on its proper page by selecting the tool when that page is showing in Hollywood's main presentation window. From the moment you create a chart, it stays bound to its page, even if you shuffle the order of the pages in the Outliner or in Presentation View. Just like all other objects.

The moment you select one of the data chart tools, Hollywood deposits you right on the front step of the Data Manager. Here, your job is to enter all the data about your subject and, when you're finished, to

Options apply to one data chart. Color schemes apply to all data charts.

Each data chart is linked to one of the presentation's pages and to a data table.

highlight only the data you want on the chart. When you use the Draw Chart command (on the File menu), Hollywood depicts the highlighted data in a chart on the current page. Its job done, the Data Manager window closes up, but the table of data you created inside the Data Manager remains with the chart behind the scenes.

Changing the Look of the Chart

The look of a data chart (just like the look of any object) is governed by two sets of controls: the presentation's color scheme and that chart's options. The color scheme makes the same changes to each and every data chart. Each chart has its very own options settings you can adjust.

You'll find that different types of data charts have different sets of options. Pie charts have slices, so one of their options lets you determine how far a slice will be slid away from the rest of the pie. Column charts have bars that run either vertically or horizontally. One column chart option determines which way they run.

Data Chart Rules

1. The options and color scheme determine its appearance.
2. The options set the characteristics of elements unique to one data chart.
3. The color scheme determines the overall design of elements common to all data charts.
4. The page upon which the chart is started determines its placement in the presentation.
5. The data table for the chart determines its content.

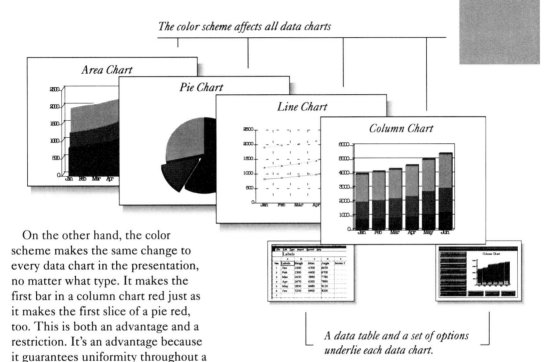

The color scheme affects all data charts

Area Chart

Pie Chart

Line Chart

Column Chart

A data table and a set of options underlie each data chart.

On the other hand, the color scheme makes the same change to every data chart in the presentation, no matter what type. It makes the first bar in a column chart red just as it makes the first slice of a pie red, too. This is both an advantage and a restriction. It's an advantage because it guarantees uniformity throughout a presentation. It's a restriction because you can't change the appearance of an individual chart by modifying the color scheme without changing every chart in the presentation.

You'll take a thorough look at color schemes in another chapter. In this chapter, you'll focus in on changing individual data chart options. But before you get that chance, you'll need to know how to select the type of data chart to use, how to supply the chart's data, and how to tell Hollywood to generate the chart. The next several pages describe these steps. ★

Your Map to the Stars

1. Choosing the right data chart and ways to start a chart: pages 39 through 42.

2. Entering and editing the chart's data: pages 43 through 48.

3. Having Hollywood draw the actual chart: pages 49 and 50.

4. Changing the chart's appearance by changing its Options: pages 51 through 56.

5. Saving your own chart designs in the Toolbox and Chart Gallery: pages 57 and 58.

Casting Call: Choosing the Right Data Chart

Each of the basic chart styles available in Hollywood specializes in communicating a particular story. Select a chart style after you've figured out the story your numbers tell.

Column Charts

Column charts are sometimes called bar charts. Each bar in a column chart shows an individual

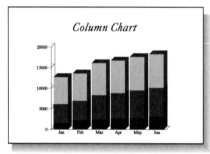

number at a specific time. Bars that are side by side make comparing individual numbers easy, which is why column charts are best for side-by-side comparisons. ("Here's how many sleigh bells we sold in December of last year versus December of the year before.")

Area Charts

Area charts have attributes of both column charts and line charts, which are described next. They show individual measurements, but also emphasize the trend from one measurement to the next. When area charts are stacked, they show how numbers change over time in

proportion to the total. ("Here are the sales figures for our four divisions

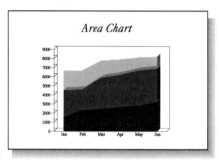

over the last six months. Notice the steady growth and percentage increase shown by the East Coast group.")

Line Charts

Line charts show progress from one point to the next, so they are best for showing growth, decline, or stability. ("Here's how our sales have

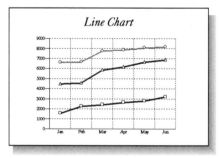

progressed over the last six months." "In this chart, you can see how we've been able to hold the line against increasing costs.")

Pie Charts

Pie charts break down a total figure to show the relative size of each segment. Each slice is one

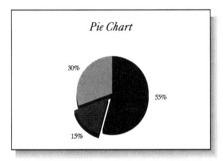
Pie Chart

component and is drawn in proportion to the other components. ("Here's our breakdown of the year's expenses, by category. Notice that my salary is a tiny slice compared to the cost of the phone system.") Two or more pies side by side show different breakdowns. ("Here's how we could increase salaries if we ripped out the phones.") They can also show the relative sizes of two overall totals when side-by-side pie charts are "proportional" (when the actual size of each pie on the page reflects the size of the total figure it represents).

Mixed Column and Line Charts

Mixed column and line charts combine the capabilities of these two chart styles. They can compare figures over an interval and show trends at the same time. "Here are our sales figures for the first three

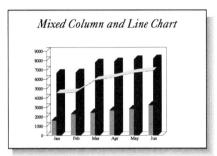
Mixed Column and Line Chart

months and here is the sales trend we predicted.")

High-Low-Close Charts

High-low-close charts are for stock watchers. They chart a day's high, low, and closing stock price.

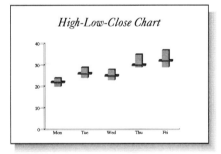
High-Low-Close Chart

("Santa's Bells, Inc. opened at 17 1/2 on Monday, hit a high of 19, and closed at 18 3/4.") They are also handy for charting any other measurement that has a high and low during an interval, such as the temperature. ★

Starting a Data Chart

Now that you've figured out the meaning behind your numbers, and selected a chart style that can express it, you're ready to start the chart. First, make sure you're viewing the page you want the chart to be on. Remember: your chart stays bound to the page in your presentation where it was first created (though you can always relocate the page).

You can choose charts from two places in Hollywood. The Toolbox is the quickest, but that's because it gives you a limited palette to work with. The Chart Gallery, with its larger palette and greater flexibility, in the long run will help you be more creative.

Rummaging in Your Toolbox

The Toolbox, on the left side of the screen, stores one predesigned chart for each of the six basic types:

a pie chart, a line chart, and so on. Just click on the Data Charts drawer in the Toolbox and you'll see a miniature picture of each one. Then click on the one you want and Hollywood gets set to create the default chart for that style with all of its options preset. All it needs now is some data, which you'll supply next in the Data Manager.

Fortunately, the defaults for each chart type in the Toolbox are not set in stone. Changing them is easy.

That means you can revise each basic chart to your own design and store *it* in the Toolbox instead, to use as a starting point for your charts. You'll learn how to set up your own default chart styles later in this chapter.

Browsing Through the Gallery

The Chart Gallery, one of Hollywood's most helpful features, gives you greater flexibility because

for each type of chart, it offers you a *handful* of versions, each with its options set differently. Among the column charts, for example, you'll find one with its bars horizontal and another with the options set for vertical. By clicking on one of these samples, you can use that chart style and its options settings for a new chart.

Eventually, you'll want to create your own chart styles and add them to the Gallery for future browsing. Adding your own chart styles is easy. You just copy a completed chart and paste it into the Gallery. You'll learn exactly how at the end of this chapter. As you begin using Hollywood, though, you'll do fine selecting from the styles provided with Hollywood. Each one is a useful and familiar permutation that will get you on the road.

▼

The Data Charts drawer in the Toolbox holds one default for each of the six basic data chart styles.

▼

You can add your own chart styles to the Chart Gallery.

▼

The Chart Gallery displays sample charts from which you can choose.

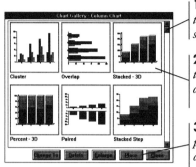

1. *Use this scroll bar to scroll down and see more chart styles.*

2. *Click on one of these boxes to select the chart style it displays.*

3. *Then, click here to place the chart on the current presentation page.*

The Chart Gallery

1. *Click here to see the available data charts.*

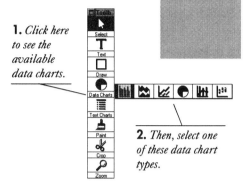

2. *Then, select one of these data chart types.*

The Data Charts Drawer

Toolbox or Chart Gallery: Where Do I Start?

Where to do your shopping depends on how you use Hollywood. If there's a particular style of chart you know you'll use a lot, you can save it as a readily available default in the Toolbox. If you use several different varieties of a particular chart type, depending on the occasion, you can keep them *all* in the Chart Gallery. Browsing through the Gallery may take a moment or two longer than starting from the Toolbox, but you'll already be several steps ahead because all of the chart's options will be set.

If you're new to Hollywood, you may want to use the Chart Gallery to become familiar with the chart styles available. You can always modify the options of any of the Gallery charts and then save your custom version alongside the original. ★

Six Easy Steps to a Chart

1. View the page where the chart should go.
2. Select a chart type from the Chart Gallery or the Toolbox.
3. Enter the numbers into a data table (or import them from a spreadsheet).
4. Highlight the numbers to chart.
5. Use Draw Chart to tell Hollywood to generate the chart.
6. Modify the chart's options, if you want.

▶ That's it. You've already done steps 1 and 2. The rest of this chapter covers steps 3 through 6 in detail.

What Is the Data Manager?

Behind every good chart lies a good table of numbers, and that table is born and lives in the Data Manager.

Once you've selected a chart style, Hollywood pops open the Data Manager window and spreads before you a blank data table, ready to receive all the numbers you want to chart. You can type them in, or you can import them from a spreadsheet created by Lotus 1-2-3 or Microsoft Excel. Either way, with the numbers in place, you're free to revise them, vary their order, or change their format — for example, changing how many decimal points the chart will show. All these operations are explained later in this chapter.

Hollywood can transform whichever numbers you wish into a chart — as easily as click, drag, press. Simply highlight a rectangular block of numbers in the data table (click on one corner of the rectangle, hold the mouse button, and drag to the opposite corner of the rectangle), then choose Draw Chart from the File menu. Hollywood does the rest. It reads in the data you've highlighted and spits out a chart of the style you chose. Almost instantly, you're looking at a finished chart on the page before you.

You can use the same data table to create more than one chart. Just save the table (use Save on the Data Manager's File menu). Whenever you want to make a different chart from the table, open the table (use Open on the Data Manager's File menu), highlight the numbers you want to chart, and use Draw Chart just as you did when you created the first chart. That saves you from having to type the same data all over again into a second data table. A data table is stored by Hollywood in a file that has a .TBL filename extension.

▼

The data for data charts resides in the Data Manager.

▼

You can import data into the Data Manager from a number-crunching spreadsheet program.

▼

Data tables are like spreadsheets without the calculating ability.

Do I Need to Save Each Data Table?

There's no need to save a data table unless you plan to create another chart from it right away. Because Hollywood needs a table of numbers in order to make a chart, each time you create a table and use Draw Chart, Hollywood asks whether it can save the table. Say "Yes" only if you want to create another chart from it right away.

When you save a presentation, Hollyood saves all of it: every page, all of the charts on every page, and all of the data tables the charts are based on. It all gets stored right in the main presentation file. You can always go back to a data table and save it separately later, if you wish. So why clutter up your disk with extra data tables unless you need to?

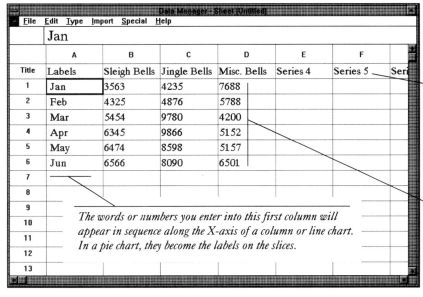

Data tables have a series name at the top of each column except the first.

A series is a sequence of numbers that measure something, usually at set intervals of time. This series measures the monthly sales of Miscellaneous Bells, for example.

The Data Manager

How Data Tables Are Organized

If you're familiar with spreadsheet software such as Excel or Lotus 1-2-3, you're already familiar with Hollywood data tables: they hold rows and columns of numbers. A data tables doesn't have a spreadsheet's ability to perform mathematical calculations on the numbers, but it *can* help you move the numbers around and change how they look. Some of these changes affect the appearance of the data table only, not the final chart: you can make numbers below a certain value red in the table and numbers above a different value green (the numbers in between stay black). Other changes affect how numbers look in both places: dollar signs in front of numbers show that they are currency, both in the data table and in the chart.

Why format the appearance of numbers in the data table? Because by studying the raw data in the data table you may uncover patterns in the numbers. Formatting all negative numbers to come out red might help you spot any deficits during fiscal periods. Then you might decide to make a chart that highlights those deficits. ★

61

Entering Numbers into the Data Manager

The terms scattered around the Data Manager window—words like "Series" and "Labels"—may not exactly come across as warm and friendly. But despite their drab sound, their meanings are specific and to the point, which is what you really need to understand the Data Manager.

Each vertical column of the data table (except the first one) can hold a series of numbers entered by you, one number below another. The numbers in a column are all related, which is why they're headed with the word "Series." One series might be the month-by-month sales of your sleigh bells; or perhaps it's a day-by-day measurement of returns.

In the first column — the one headed "Labels" instead — you type in words or dates that will end up along the X-axis (usually the horizontal axis) of your finished chart. Often, these are intervals of time (January, February, March...). If you're making a pie chart, the labels will be the names of the pie slices instead.

Column Headings

The headings atop the columns ("Series 1," "Series 2") do more than just identify the columns. Unless you change them, they will appear as is in the legend of your finished chart. Most likely you'll want more descriptive terms on your chart — "Marketing Expenses," perhaps, or

"Salaries" — which tell your viewers a whole lot more about what the numbers mean than "Series 1" and "Series 2." Changing them is easy. Just type the new names right over the old.

If you got to the Data Manager by choosing to start a new pie chart rather than a bar chart, you'll see that the columns are labeled "Pie 1," "Pie 2," and so on. Each column becomes a different pie, and the numbers in each column determine the size of each slice in that pie. You'll want to replace these names with something more descriptive, too.

You'll notice that there are series names at the top of the first eight columns. You wouldn't want to use them all, though. Two, three, or four series is normal for a chart. Five or six series starts to get a bit complicated. And seven or eight would put the chart — and your viewers — into absolute overload. If you really have to compare that many series of numbers, consider breaking them into two groups. That way you can display several in one chart and the rest in a second chart. Remember, your goal in charting is to create a device that tells a story quickly and clearly. If your viewer ends up struggling to sort out a complex chart, the point of charting is lost: You might just as well present the raw numbers.

▼

Enter a related set of numbers in one of the columns with a "Series" label at the top.

▼

Enter the labels for the X-axis in the first column.

Easy Entry

The simplest way to fill in a blank column with a series of numbers is to first position the cursor on the column's topmost available space; you can do this with either the arrow keys or the mouse. Next, type in a number and press the down arrow on the keyboard. Now, with the cursor on the cell below, type another number, and press the down arrow again if you need to continue. This way, you don't have to press Enter after you type each entry, although you do have to press Enter to enter the last number at the bottom of the column.

To change a number, simply put the cursor on it and type a new one right over the old. Or, you can put the cursor on it, press F2 (Edit), and then revise the current entry, which shows up in the status line near the top of the Data Manager window. When you've made the change you need, press Enter to enter the revision.

Using One Table for Several Charts

If you're planning to create several similar charts on one subject, you may find it helpful to enter all of your data for that subject into a single data table. That way you can get the work of data entry out of the way and then base each chart on data from a different part of the same table.

Let's say you have monthly sales figures for five years. That's sixty numbers. And, you want to create a separate chart for each year. You can get the entry work over with by entering all sixty numbers into a single data table and then using Save on the File menu to save it on disk. Later, when you start each chart, you can use Open on the File menu to retrieve the saved data table. For each chart, you'll highlight the data for that year before using Draw Chart on the File menu to generate the chart. You'll learn all about Draw Chart later in this chapter. ★

Generating Labels Automatically

Typing a list of labels into the first column of a data table can be pure drudgery, so why not let Hollywood do it for you? First, highlight as many rectangular cells in the first column as

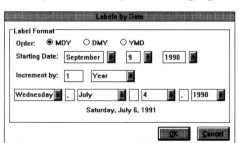

you want filled with labels (twelve if you want "Jan" through "Dec", for example). Then, select Generate Labels... from the Special menu. Choose the type of label you want next (Number, Date, or Quarter) and then supply the information Hollywood requests in the next dialog box. Keep your eye on the example at the bottom center of the dialog box. It shows you how the choices you make affect a sample label.

Importing Numbers from a Spreadsheet

Copying numbers from a Lotus 1-2-3 or Excel worksheet into a Hollywood data table sure beats typing them all over again. After all, why not let Hollywood handle the work when, for example, you want to maintain numbers in a spreadsheet program for calculating and have a duplicate set in Hollywood for graphing?

There are other times when you might need to import numbers from a spreadsheet, too. Some people have programs that download numbers from a mainframe into a 1-2-3 WK1 file. Others periodically gather numbers that arrive in worksheets from field offices.

The Data Manager makes it easy to lift data for a data table from a worksheet by displaying both the worksheet and the data table on the screen side by side. On the left, you can highlight numbers in the worksheet, and on the right, you can point to a destination in the data table for the copies. Then, Import Data on the Import menu does the trick, copying what you've highlighted from the left to the right.

Starting an Import

To start the import process, you select Open Source... on the Import menu. A dialog box prompts you to choose between importing data from a Microsoft Excel XLS file or a Lotus 1-2-3 WK1 file and it gives you a scrollbar so you can select the correct worksheet file on disk. After you select a worksheet, Hollywood retrieves and displays it in a window on the left. In a window on the right, it displays the current data table. That data table is probably still blank, but you're about to change that.

If the numbers in the worksheet you want happen to fall in a vertical column, your job is easy. You just highlight the column of numbers in the worksheet, then click on the topmost blank space in the first available column on the right, except the very first. Column number one (it has the word "Labels" at the top) is reserved for X-axis labels (more on those a little later). You don't need to highlight an entire destination area in the data table. Just clicking on the topmost cell will do.

When you've got the correct data highlighted on the left and the correct destination highlighted on the right, select Import Data from the Import menu. You'll see your numbers copy from left to right in a flash. After that successful round, you're ready to copy more. You can go back to the worksheet on the left and highlight another column and repeat the process if you want. You can even copy several side-by-side columns from the worksheet at the same time by highlighting them all. You still need to select only a single space as the destination in the data table. The columns of numbers will start pouring into the data table at that space and lay out side by side, just as they were in the worksheet.

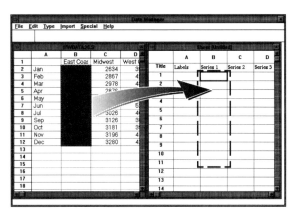

Importing a column of numbers from an Excel worksheet

Importing the Heading, Too

If you also highlight the heading of a column of numbers in the worksheet, you can select one of the headings in the data table ("Series 1," "Series 2," and so on) as a destination rather than selecting the first blank space. When you then import the data, the worksheet column headings overlay the "Series 1," "Series 2" headings and you've automatically got series names that are far more descriptive. If you don't import headings from the worksheet, you'll want to take a minute to type over "Series 1," "Series 2," and so on with names that adequately describe the series.

What If My Numbers Are in Rows?

If the numbers in your worksheet lie in horizontal rows rather than columns, you'll need to take an extra step once the data is in Hollywood. This maneuver rearranges the rows into columns.

After you import one or several rows, you need to convert the rows of numbers into columns by using the Swap Rows/Columns command on the Edit menu. You'll learn about this command next. ★

Importing Data From Several Sources

You can pull data into one data table from several different sources. Some of it you might need to type in manually. But, you can also pull some from one worksheet, then open another worksheet and pull some more from that, and so on, pulling different sets of numbers from as many worksheets as you want.

Each time you use Open Source..., the Data Manager displays the current data table on the right, which shows whatever data it already holds. Select a worksheet, highlight data in the worksheet, and then copy in the data next to or below the data already in the data table.

Swapping and Switching Columns and Rows

Until now, you've found it easy to import numbers from a worksheet into your Hollywood data table — but what's this? The worksheet's numbers run across in rows rather than down in columns. Hollywood can handle it. It just takes an extra step.

Normally, when you type numbers into the Data Manager, you enter them one below another in columns. Hollywood expects to find a related series of numbers in a column, and it tells you so by putting a series name at the top of each column (except the very first, which is reserved for X-axis labels). But when you go into a worksheet for the numbers you need, you may find them in rows instead. Go ahead and import them into your data table anyway. They can be automatically rearranged into columns by using Swap Columns/Rows on the Edit menu.

Your first step is to highlight the rectangular region in the data table where the swap will take place: the rows you're lifting *and* the columns where you're laying them back down. Swap Columns/Rows then takes the first row of highlighted numbers and places it in the first highlighted column. The next row then moves to the column to the

right of the first, and so on. Almost instantly, a group of rows is transposed into columns.

The key to swapping rows for columns is to highlight all the way across the rows in the data table and then to highlight down just as far. If your rows contain twelve numbers across, make sure you highlight all twelve and then also highlight down twelve rows, too. The final highlighted rectangle should be the same number of columns wide as it is rows tall. Only when this condition is met does Swap Columns/Rows become available on the Edit menu.

More Rows, Please

But what if you've already got several columns of numbers in a data table and you need to pull in a few more rows of numbers? The best way is to import them into a remote area of the data table, away from the columns you already have. Then, use Swap Columns/Rows out there. After that, you can cut and paste the columns where you want them. The sidebar on the right — "Please Pass the Rows" — tells you how.

The Big Switch

Switch Columns/Rows, also on the Edit menu, is a similar maneuver. It switches one entire column with the column immediately to its right, or one entire row with the row below it.

With this command, you can change the order of the series in a chart. Suppose you've got the sales

---

To transform rows of numbers from a worksheet into columns, use the Swap command after you've imported the rows into a data table.

Edit	
Undo Swap Row/Col	Alt+Bksp
Cut	Sh+Del
Copy	Ctl+Ins
Paste	Sh+Ins
Clear	Del
Insert Row/Column	
Delete Row/Column	
Switch Rows/Columns	
Swap Rows/Columns	
Merge Cells	
Un-Merge Cells	
Use Color Scheme	

Switching columns or rows lets you change the order of series in the chart.

Before Swap

After Swap

Swapping Columns/Rows

Click here to highlight the entire B column, which will switch with column C to the right.

Make sure this highlighted area is as many rows tall as it is columns wide.

Before — — *After*

Switching Columns/Rows

figures for ten different divisions — Division I, Division II, and so on — laid out in that order in your data table. With Switch Columns/Rows you can reorder them from lowest sales to highest, giving you a final chart that instantly shows your viewers who's doing better than whom.

To switch two columns, first click on the letter at the very top of a column to highlight the entire column quickly. Then, use Switch Columns/Rows on the Edit menu. The highlighted column switches with the column to its right. Highlight two columns instead, and they switch with the two columns to their right. If you click on a number at the left of one of the rows, Switch Columns/Rows will switch that row with the one below it.

If you need to move a column or row somewhere else entirely, cutting and pasting does the job. ★

Please Pass the Rows

The Edit menu holds some more things you can do with entire rows and columns, or just with parts of them. Any rectangle of numbers you highlight is removed when you use Cut, leaving the empty cells in place. You can bring the numbers back somewhere else — in empty cells or right on top of some old numbers — by putting the cursor there and then using Paste. Copy works the same, but it doesn't remove the numbers you highlight.

To insert a blank column, highlight the column that is now where you want the new one to appear; for a new row, highlight just where the new row should go. Then Insert Row/Column does what its name says, moving everything to the right or down to make room. To delete a row or column, highlight it and use Delete Row/Column.

Formatting Data Tables

Changing the appearance of a data table, or of the numbers and text it contains, can help you in two ways. It can make the data table easier to interpret — a great help should someone other than yourself want a look at the numbers behind one of your charts. It also lets you change the formatting of data point labels — those little numbers that can appear on a finished chart right next to the bars or slices, indicating their numeric value.

Formatting the Table

Probably the most useful change to a data table is to alter the widths of the columns and the heights of the rows so they can accommodate extra-wide or extra-tall entries. You'll probably change the column widths most often. The easiest way is to click and drag on the small vertical lines between the letters at the tops of the columns. You can make the first column wider by placing the cursor on the vertical line between "A" and "B" and then holding the mouse button down while dragging to the right. The rest of the table moves over to make room. To change the height of a row, drag down the small horizontal line between the row numbers at the left side of the table.

Another way to make these changes is on the Special menu, where Column Width and Row Height let you type in exact measurements for whichever columns or rows are highlighted.

Display, also on the Special menu, lets you turn off the display of column and row headings and the grid lines in the table. You may want to suppress headings and grid lines before printing a data table.

To change the color of the numbers in your data table or of the cells that hold them, highlight the cells you want changed and then select Color from the Special menu (or you can press F6). Select Text to change the color of text, or Fill to change the color of the cell background. Then, select a color from the Color dialog box and select Apply.

Formatting Text

Any text you type into a data table (series names or X-axis labels) will appear in the default text style unless you specify otherwise. To change its appearance, highlight it and then pull down the Type menu. The easiest change is to pick a different *style* for it with Styles. You'll learn all about setting up styles for text in Chapter 6. But you can also select and change any of the other text attributes shown on the Type menu (Bold, Italic, Underline,

[Special menu shown: Color... F6, Number..., Generate Labels..., Display..., Row Height..., Column Width..., Cell Margins..., Get Range..., Save Range..., Arrange by Tiling, Arrange by Stacking]

[Type menu shown: Plain, Bold, Italic, Underline, All Caps, Small Caps, Font, Size, Justification, Styles, Define Styles...]

Click and drag on one of these vertical lines between column headings to change the width of a column.

Or, click on one of these horizontal lines to change the height of a row.

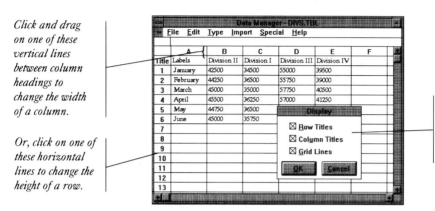

This Display dialog box pops up when you select Display from the Special menu.

The Data Manager with the Display Dialog Box Showing

Use these controls to change the formatting of...

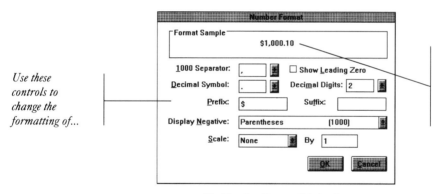

...this sample number, which shows how numbers will look both in the data table and in the chart.

The Number Format Dialog Box

Size). Remember, the key is to first highlight the text to change, and then to pick formatting for it from the Type menu.

Formatting Numbers

If you decide to have the numbers from your data table also appear as data point labels in your finished chart, whatever format you select for the numbers in the data table will govern the chart as well. You change the format of numbers by highlighting them, and then using

Numbers on the Special menu. The Format Numbers dialog box will appear, showing a sample formatted number at the top. Below that are the controls you can use to change the sample number's format. If your numbers are dollar figures, you can type in a $ as a prefix and change the decimal value to 2. (The "Auto" decimal value leaves your numbers as entered.) When you're done, all the numbers you've highlighted in the data table will look like the sample number at the top of the Format Numbers dialog box. ★

Drawing the Chart

At this point, the quick and easy jump from a completed data table to a drawn data chart is just a single menu command away. Draw Chart on the File menu does just what it says: It draws the chart you've chosen and places it on the current presentation page. But first, you have to highlight the numbers you want to include in the chart.

File	
New	Ctrl+N
Open...	Ctrl+O
Save	Ctrl+S
Save As...	
Change Printer...	
Print...	Ctrl+P
Draw Chart...	
Chart Options...	
Exit	

Say you want to include a block of several side-by-side columns. Start by highlighting the word "Labels" at the top of the leftmost column, plus all the series names above the columns you want in the chart. Then, highlight all the way down the rightmost column you want included, until you reach the last numbers you want in the chart. The entire rectangle will become highlighted. (By including the leftmost column, you've made sure the labels you entered there will appear along the chart's X-axis.)

You don't have to highlight every number in each column, by the way; just the columns you want and the numbers you need. You can highlight only the first three columns and only the first twelve numbers in each, for example.

If you want to highlight columns that are not beside one another — the first and third series, for example — highlight the first column and then press and hold the Shift key while highlighting the third column. This lets you highlight several noncontiguous regions. You can highlight any series and any rows, but if you highlight even a single number in a series, make sure the series heading at the top of the column is highlighted, too. The same goes for rows: Highlight any number in a row, and the label in the first column should be highlighted, too. Otherwise, your chart may not be what you expected.

Positioning the Chart

After you select Draw Chart, Hollywood positions the chart on the presentation page according to rules stored in the *template* you are using for the current presentation. We'll look at templates in Chapter 8.

If the chart is not just where you want it, though, repositioning it is easy enough. To move the whole thing, position the mouse pointer at the center of the chart and click on the mouse button. Small black frame handles will surround the chart, telling you the chart has been selected. Now just press and hold the mouse button and drag the chart to the spot you like.

To change the width or height of your chart, click and hold on one of

▼

Highlight the numbers in the data table that you want charted and then select Draw Chart.

▼

Highlight any number in a data table, and the corresponding column heading and row label should be highlighted, too.

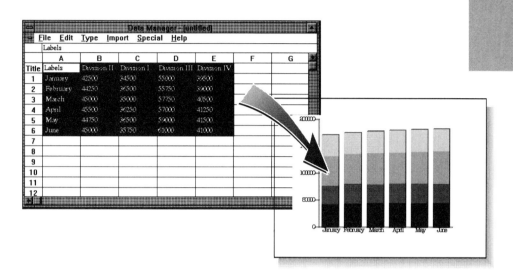

From Data to Data Chart with the Draw Chart Command

the frame handles and move the side up or down, in or out. If you want the *entire* chart smaller or larger, you can change its size without distorting its

shape by holding down the Shift key while you drag one of the corner frame handles toward or away from the center of the chart. ★

But That's Not What I Wanted!

Oops! Despite your best intentions, the chart just drawn by Hollywood isn't exactly what you had in mind. Now is the best time to go back to the data and make changes. Simply click on the chart so that it's surrounded by frame handles, and then either press Ctrl-D or select Data Table/Outline on the Edit menu. In a moment,

you'll be right back in the Data Manager. Fix up whatever you need and then try Draw Chart again. To select a different chart type altogether, select Chart Gallery from the Special menu, choose a different chart style, and then press the Change To button at the bottom of the Chart Gallery.

Changing Data Chart Options

T he chart that Hollywood draws for you has all the same options settings as the model chart you selected from the Chart Gallery or from the Data Charts drawer of the Toolbox. Remember that a chart's options control the features unique to that chart, such as the degree to which a slice of a pie chart is cut and slid away from the rest of the pie, or the thickness of the lines in a line chart. The color scheme, on the other hand, controls the features that are common to all chart types, such as the typeface of the page titles or the colors of the bars, lines, or slices representing different series.

As you read the rest of this chapter and practice with Hollywood charts, you'll soon learn which aspects of the chart are controlled by its options. Everything else you might want to change about a chart is probably controlled by the color scheme. There's no option to change the typeface of the chart titles, for example; that's because — as you'll learn in Chapter 8 — data chart titles are controlled by the color scheme instead.

Sometimes, you'll want to change a chart's options in order to change how it communicates its message. Other times, you'll just want to give the chart a little visual flair. If you reduce the upper and lower limits of a line chart's vertical axis, for example, the lines seem to rise and

fall less. That one simple change can alter the chart's mood from glum to cheery — or the other way around. On the other hand, giving a pie chart a 3D effect is purely a move to enhance its appeal; it doesn't really increase the chart's ability to communicate (although increasing its appeal may in fact enhance its powers to persuade).

Calling Up Options

To change the options of any chart, double-click on the chart (double-clicking on any object shows you the options for that object, if it has any) or select the chart and use Options on the View menu. In a moment, a large dialog box shows you a miniature of the chart on the right and, on the left, a series of buttons you can press to choose different groups of options. You can change as many options as you wish, or change only a single option for just a minor alteration. When you've made all of the changes you need, select OK in the main options dialog box. If you decide not to change any options for the chart, select Cancel instead.

If you select the chart by clicking on it just once, and then return to the Chart Gallery (on the Special menu), you can select a different chart type altogether. Or, you can select a different variation of the same chart type. A different variation gives you a different set of options for the same chart. The chart will be redrawn

---

Double-click on a chart to begin changing its options.

If you can't find an option to change an aspect of the chart's appearance, it's probably controlled by the color scheme.

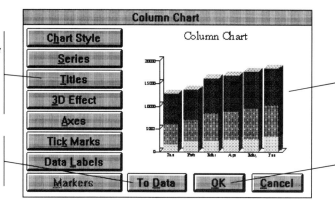

Press any of these buttons to pop open a dialog box with options settings you can change for the current chart.

This miniature of the current chart shows you changes to the options settings as you make them.

Click here to return to the chart's data table in the Data Manager.

Click here to register all of the options changes you have made.

The Main Options Dialog Box

using whatever options settings are shown by the sample chart.

Back to the Data

There's one selection in the options dialog box that's not about setting options at all. Suppose you discover some of your data needs changing: To Data takes you back to the chart's data table in the Data Manager. There, you can make changes to the

numbers underlying the chart, after which Draw Chart will create the revised chart. Another way to get to the data table is to click on the chart and then either press Ctrl-D (for data) or select Data Table/Outline from the View menu.

The next several sets of pages take a look at all of the options you can change. ★

The Color Scheme's Role in Formatting Data Charts

You'll be learning about color schemes in depth in Chapter 8, but for now, here are the components of data charts that you format by changing the presentation's color scheme rather than changing the chart's options:

1. Axes Background
2. Chart Title and Footnote
3. Data Point Labels
4. Grid Color

5. Legend Frame and Title
6. Color, Fill Pattern, or Color Wash of Each Series
7. X-Axis, Y1-Axis, and Y2-Axis Titles

Data Chart Options: Chart Style

After you've summoned the data chart options dialog box by double-clicking on a data chart, you next select one of the eight categories of options shown in the dialog box. Chart Style is the first of these and it's the subject of this section.

Selecting Chart Style leads to another dialog box; it shows a set of chart style options that fit the type of chart you're creating. The Chart Style dialog boxes for each chart type are pictured here on these two pages. The easiest way to become familiar with the options in these dialog boxes is to examine the sample charts in the Chart Gallery as you read this section.

Try selecting Chart Gallery on the Special menu. As you scroll through the Chart Gallery, you'll see first the seven basic column charts Hollywood provides. Then, if you continue to scroll down, you'll see six area charts, followed by five line charts, two pie charts, three mixed charts, and three high-low-close charts. Among the sample charts in the Gallery, you'll find examples of most of the chart style options described here.

Column Chart Styles

The chart style labeled Cluster in the Chart Gallery is the same as the one called Regular in the Chart Style dialog box. Its bars are clustered around each X-axis point. The Overlap chart overlaps the bars

clustered around each X-axis point. (In this case, the bars run in a horizontal direction; which way they run can be changed using Direction in the Chart Style dialog box.) The Stacked chart accumulates the values at each X-axis point and piles them on top of one another. The stacking helps show the grand total for each X-axis point in addition to showing the breakdown at each point. The Percent chart looks like a stacked chart, but it shows only the percentage each value contributes to the total (the total of values at each X-axis point is 100%). The Paired chart draws the first two series on opposite axes. The Stacked Step chart is a stacked chart with 0% space between the bars rather than the built-in 25%.

Overlap Amount, in the Chart Style dialog box, sets the degree of overlap of side-by-side bars. Space Between determines the amount of blank space between sets of bars.

Area Chart Styles

The chart styles available for area charts are much simpler. You can see  from the Chart Gallery that the styles labeled Regular, Stacked Step, and Percentage are just like their column chart counterparts.

▼

A series of options in the Chart Styles dialog box with round buttons next to them present either/or options. You must choose one of these options.

▼

An option with a square next to it may be selected in addition to the other options.

Line Chart Styles

In the Regular line chart, the lines run from one data point in a series to the next. The Stacked Step line chart  uses both horizontal and vertical lines to connect points. The Scatter line chart, despite being called a line chart, has no lines. (Statisticians often call scatter charts either scatterplots or scattergrams.) Show with Markers, in the dialog box, places diamonds, triangles, squares, and other shapes (a different shape for each series) at the data points of any line chart. Another chart style option lets you choose among thin, medium, and thick lines for all the lines in the chart.

Pie Chart Styles

When a pie chart contains two or more pies (two or more series), Hollywood can depict the ratio  between the sum of the numbers in each pie by changing each pie's size. A proportionally larger pie means a proportionally greater sum. The Proportional Radius option sizes each pie by changing its radius.

Proportional Area changes the total area of each pie instead. To draw pies of equal size regardless of their totals, simply leave the option setting at Regular.

The slices of the pies run counterclockwise, starting at the angle you enter for Start Pie at. (The angle is measured in clock time: "12 o'clock," "3 o'clock," etc.) The slices can be arranged in the order entered into the data table (Show as Entered) or arranged in order by size (Smallest to Largest).

Mixed Column and Line Chart Styles

Mixed column and line charts have  only two chart style options: Direction (Horizontal or Vertical) and Line Width (Thin, Medium, or Thick).

High-Low-Close Chart Styles

High-low-close charts can be displayed Without Close (without the small horizontal bar that crosses the high-low column and depicts the closing value). Whether or not they show close, they can also show volume (a line plotted against the Y2- axis). The only other chart style option available here is Direction (Horizontal or Vertical). ★

Data Chart Options II, the Sequel:
Series, Titles, and 3D Effect

▼

The Progressive Build option in the Series dialog box is related to the Layers command, discussed in Chapter 9.

▼

Think of titles as advertising headlines: short and punchy.

▼

A 3D effect makes charts more appealing but doesn't change their message.

More data chart options are available under the Series, Titles, and 3D Effect buttons. Set these too, if you wish, before you select OK to return to the chart.

Series Selections

For most chart types (except pie charts and mixed column and line charts), the Series options let you assign each series in the chart to either the Y1 (left) or Y2 (right) vertical axis. (Each Y-axis can have a different numeric range, one suitable for some series and the other suitable for others.) Another Series option, Progressive Build, lets you specify the way the chart is assembled when it is "built" section by section in an animated screen show. In the chapter on screen shows, you'll learn about *builds* in detail. For now, though, just understand that when you select either By Data Sets or By Data Points, Hollywood automatically sends different parts of the chart to different layers. (Layers are much like transparent overlays. You'll learn about them, too, in the screen show chapter.) Selecting By Data Sets

sends each *series* to a different layer. Selecting By Data Points sends each *data point* to a different layer. That way, at presentation time you can progressively reveal information by adding one layer at a time.

For pie charts and mixed column and line charts, the Series options give you other choices. When you're making a pie chart, the Series options show you the color of each pie slice, and the degree to which it is exploded (cut and slid away from the rest of the pie). Explode is set in inches. And when you're making a mixed column and line chart, the Series options let you decide how each series will be represented: select either Line, Bar, or Scatter (points without connecting lines). You might, for example, choose to display the first three series with bars and the fourth series with a line.

Enlightening Titles

A good chart doesn't just have titles, it has headlines that reach out and grab you. Your titles should be short, clear, and punchy. "East Coast Revenues, Jan-Jun" adequately describes a chart, but "East Coast Posts Huge Gross"

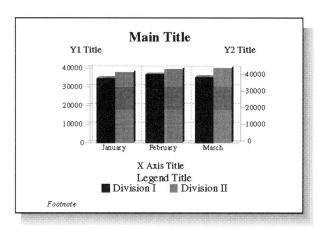

Data Chart Titles

intrigues your viewers and makes them want to take a closer look.

There are six different kinds of titles that can appear on a chart: a main title, footnote, legend title, an X-axis title, a Y1-axis title, and a Y2-axis title. To create them, first select Titles, then enter as much text as you need for each title in the boxes provided. Hollywood will let you know with a warning message if you've entered too much to fit on the chart.

Selecting OK in the Options dialog box sets your titles into place. Seeing them on the chart, you may want to make a few changes to their size, positioning, or typeface. Unfortunately, titles set in place using the options settings can't be formatted individually; rather, you'd have to modify the chart's color scheme. This, of course, makes the same change to every data chart title in your presentation — but it does

ensure that the presentation looks consistent. The drawback is a lack of flexibility.

One solution to this problem is to leave the Titles entries blank and use the Text tool instead to place free-floating titles on top of the chart. Free-floating text *can* be formatted independently. Chapter 6 describes using the Text tool in detail.

Into the Third Dimension

You just can't beat that 3D Effect for adding real pizzazz to a chart. 3D doesn't change what the chart says, but it sure enhances how the chart says it.

After you select 3D Effect and choose Turn on 3D in the 3D Effect dialog box, Horizontal and Vertical let you set the amount of 3D Effect separately for each direction. Subtle 3D effects can enhance a chart without stealing attention from its content. ★

Data Chart Options III:
Axes, Tick Marks, Data Labels and Markers

Whether or not you change any of the options under Axes, Tick Marks, Data Labels, or Markers, your charts are already quite acceptable at this point. They can become even more expressive, though, if you fine-tune these settings to clarify the message your chart tells.

Axes of Excellence

Grid lines on a chart can help a viewer to visualize the actual value that each data point represents. Y-axis grid lines run horizontally, while X-axis grid lines run vertically. Grid Lines in the Axes dialog box lets you choose whether the lines will be solid, dashed, or not appear at all. The color of the chart's background (called the Axes Background) is determined by the color scheme, instead.

Scale determines whether the scale of a Y-axis will be linear or logarithmic. Choosing Linear makes all the increments along the axis equal in value. Log makes each successive value ten times the previous one.

Axis Placement lets you switch the Y1-axis from the left side of the chart to the right, and vice versa for the Y2. It also lets you move the X-axis from the bottom of the chart to the top.

The frame of a chart is a box that encloses the active area of the chart. Full Axes surrounds the entire chart with a frame. Half Axes frames only the left and bottom sides. No Axes produces a chart that floats freely, with no frame at all.

Ticks That Don't Bite: Tick Marks

The Tick Marks dialog box shows identical, side-by-side options for the Y1 and Y2 axes only. There are no tick mark settings for the X-axis.

Maximum and Minimum let you change the upper and lower values of each axis. Normally, Hollywood enters these numbers for you, but you can override the default and set them yourself.

The increments along an axis are shown with tick marks; some are called Majors and some are Minors. Majors are labeled to show their actual value; Minors appear simply as tick marks that fall between the Majors. If you choose 1000 for the Major increments, Hollywood labels the axis at every thousand (1000, 2000, 3000, etc.). If at # of Minors you enter 3, for example, Hollywood produces three tick marks between each Major — in this case, at 250, 500, 750, and so on.

Tick marks can cross a Y-axis or jut out from it, either to the inside or the outside of the chart. Settings in the dialog box let you make these choices.

To restore the Tick Mark options to their original default settings, click on Use Defaults.

To create a chart that floats freely without a frame, select No Axes.

Decreasing the limits of the Y-axis, amplifies the appearance of change.

Data labels add precision to a chart by relating exact numbers.

Division III Achieves 2Q Goals

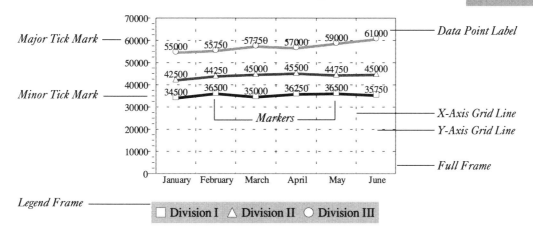

Major Tick Mark

Minor Tick Mark

Legend Frame

Data Point Label

X-Axis Grid Line
Y-Axis Grid Line

Full Frame

Markers

☐ Division I   △ Division II   ○ Division III

Data Labels

Data labels in Hollywood charts are the numbers or words that appear within the chart to identify exact data values or series names. The settings for a chart's legend also appear in this dialog box.

Data point labels are numbers within the chart that tell the actual value of the points plotted. If you select Place Inside rather than Don't Show Labels, data point labels will appear within the bars, lines, or pie slices. Place Outside makes them appear next to the bars, lines, or pie slices instead. Show Value displays the exact value of each point. Show as a Percent displays the percentage value of each point. The color and typeface of data labels are determined by the color scheme.

When you're creating a pie chart, Data Series Label becomes available.

This option lets you show the amount each slice of the pie represents, either Inside or Outside the pie.

Legend Placement lets you determine where the chart's legend appears. Unless None is selected, you can always select Show With Frame to surround the legend with a filled box. The color or color wash of the fill is determined by the color scheme.

Markers

When the chart you're creating is a line chart, Markers becomes available so you can select one of the eight marker styles for each series. Markers mark each data point along a line, but they appear only if you have already selected Show With Markers when you set the Chart Style options. ★

Setting Defaults for Data Chart Options

The Chart Gallery can hold your own model charts.

Simply copy and paste a chart into the Chart Gallery for future use.

You can change the options of any of the charts in the Toolbox, too.

T hink of it as recycling. The charts that cost you so much time and effort needn't get tossed in the garbage when you finish a presentation. They can become part of a permanent library of data chart designs you can select from whenever you need to create a new chart.

You're already familiar with the Chart Gallery, which stores model versions of each different chart type. But you haven't yet seen how to store your own work in the Chart Gallery side by side with Hollywood's starter charts. Eventually, when you need a new chart, you'll be able to scan through the frozen charts left over from last week's meal and see if there's anything you might thaw out and reuse.

You can also go into the Data Charts drawer of the Toolbox and revise the master chart stored there for each chart type. Say you always reserve the second line of the title for your company name. Why not add it to all six master charts in the Toolbox? Then, whenever you start a new chart, your company name will be there. You'll never need to type it in again.

Donating Charts to the Chart Gallery

To put a chart into the Chart Gallery, select the chart and then select Copy from the Edit menu. Then, open the Chart Gallery and select Paste from the Edit menu. Hollywood places the chart in the Gallery along with the other charts of the same type. Add a new column chart, for example, and it appears in the Gallery following all of the other column charts.

The color scheme in effect when a chart is made determines how the chart looks in the Chart Gallery. The next time you create a presentation, the Chart Gallery will still show the chart with its colorful color scheme even if you are making a presentation for a black and white printer. If you were to select that colorful chart from the Gallery, Hollywood would then create a new chart with all of the same options, but it would use the color scheme of the new presentation instead. If a color scheme for a black-and-white printer, say for a LaserJet, was attached to the new presentation, that very colorful chart might now appear in shades of gray .

If you've created a chart to *replace* one of the charts in the Gallery, you can delete the old chart by selecting it and then selecting Delete in the Chart Gallery's dialog box.

Revising the Toolbox Data Charts

The master chart designs stored in the Toolbox are subject to revision whenever you feel like it. Would you like your name in the footnote of every chart you create? No problem. Just enter your name in the Footnote option of each master chart in the Toolbox.

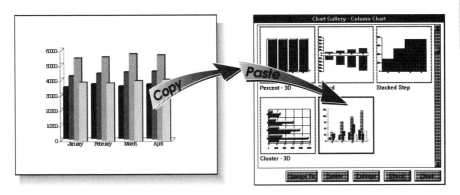

Copying a Finished Chart to the Chart Gallery

To revise a chart style, open the Data Charts drawer in the Toolbox. Then, be sure to press and hold the Control (Ctrl) key while you select one of the six chart styles. In a minute, the main Options dialog box for that chart style will appear. Go ahead and make any changes to the options you want. Then, select OK to record your changes permanently. The next time you make a chart of that type, you'll see its new option settings in effect. ★

Where To from Here?

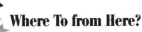

✔ 1. Starting and Outlining
     a Presentation
✔ 2. Adding Bullet and Data Charts
Next: 3. Adding Other Chart Types
    4. Adding the Trimmings:
      Extra Text and Graphics
    5. Making Changes
    6. Recording the Design
    7. Showing Off Your Work

Congratulations! You've made it through the most exacting part of this book. By now, you should be able to start a presentation, outline its structure, and add both bullet and data charts. Before you're through, you'll also need to learn how to add the other chart types Hollywood makes and how to add additional text and graphics to spruce up the basic design. When the basic presentation is in order, you'll learn how to revise the color scheme and establish a template so you can reuse your design in future presentations.

Next up: how to create the supporting players: table and tree charts.

The SUPPORTING PLAYERS

Adding Table and Tree Charts

In This Chapter

◆

Introducing Table and Tree Charts

Maybe not as popular as bullet and data charts, but certainly no less useful, Hollywood table and tree charts are perfect for telling two types of stories that bullet and data charts just can't relate as well: side-by-side comparisons and the structure of organizations.

Table charts show side-by-side columns of text.

Table Manners

Table charts arrange statements of a few words each in side-by-side columns for easy comparison. One table, for example, might compare consumer attitudes about seven leading home care products, with the product names running down the left side of the table, attitudes expressed by males placed in the middle, and attitudes expressed by females on the right. Another table might contain just two columns: pros on the left and cons on the right.

Table charts also can show tables of numbers, but they were designed primarily for text, so you won't see the decimal points of numbers neatly aligned under one another as you might like. With experience, you'll come up with your own uses for Hollywood table charts, and you're sure to find table charts as easy to make as all Hollywood charts.

You can use a table chart to show a table of numbers, but the decimal points won't line up properly.

Tree charts diagram a hierarchical structure.

A Tree Grows in Hollywood

Tree charts diagram any hierarchical structure — the organization of a corporation, say, or of a bureaucracy — any structure that has various subordinate levels to it. In fact, they are often called "organization charts" or just "org charts."

The tree chart for your company might show the company president's name in a box at the top, several vice presidents in boxes below, and several managers in boxes below each vice president's box. Lines link the boxes to show who reports to whom.

Tree charts also can be handy for detailing tasks and subtasks, or for creating a flow chart or timeline for a project. By flipping the tree on its side and turning the connecting lines into arrows, you can diagram a process and its inputs along a path toward a goal.

Building Tables and Planting Trees

Both table and tree charts are text charts, so you'll find their icons if you rummage through the Text Charts drawer of the Toolbox. And, both are like data charts in that they're tacked on to presentation pages you've already made. That means there's no need to interrupt the planning of your presentation outline just to design them. Simply reserve spots for them

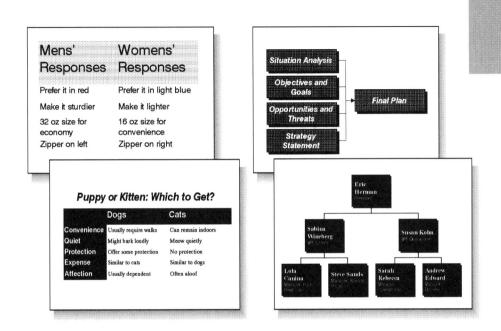

Some Hollywood Table and Tree Chart Samples

on the appropriate pages of the outline, and then go back later to do the design work.

When you start a table chart (by selecting the table chart icon), you're taken to the Data Manager. The data table you create there will become a table chart on the current presentation page. When you start a tree chart, on the other hand, it's the Outliner that pops up; the same Outliner in which you create the main presentation outline. The outline structure you enter, with its topmost level, levels indented below, and other levels indented still further, becomes the pattern of the branches of the tree.

Collections of Objects

Both table and tree charts go onto presentation pages as objects, just like anything else that goes onto the pages of a Hollywood presentation. But, unlike a data chart, which is a single object, a table or tree chart can be composed of many objects, each with its own options. Each leaf and each line in a tree chart, for example, can have its own options settings. Learning how to customize the options of these objects will let you get just the table or tree chart you need. You'll learn about changing the options of table and tree charts later in this chapter. First, you should know how to supply the content of each chart type; that's covered in the next two pages. ★

Setting Up a Table Chart

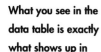

A table chart is a Hollywood data table formatted and placed on a page.

What you see in the data table is exactly what shows up in the table chart.

As long as you recall that table charts are a kind of text chart, you'll remember where to go to start one: into the Text Charts drawer of the Toolbox where you'll select the table chart icon inside. Immediately, you're taken to the Data Manager, where a blank data table awaits. Your first job is to supply the data for the data table. Then, if you want, you can format the appearance of the data table to spruce up the appearance of the final table chart. Finally, you'll transform the data table into a table chart with just a few simple steps.

To enter data for the chart, you need to know how to handle the Data Manager. You learned about the Data Manager in Chapter 4, the one on creating data charts. If it's been a while since you've looked at that chapter, or since you've used the Data Manager, you might want to review the information there. You'll find it helpful as you work through this chapter, too.

Setting Up the Data Table

The data table you create for a table chart is similar to one for a data chart, except that it doesn't require row headings along its left side and column headings along its top. You might get by with one or the other. If the table is meant to provide comments about three topics, for example, you can place three column headings at the top and put three columns of comments into cells

below. You won't need row headings.

After entering the column or row headings, you should now enter the text statements you want to make, each in its own cell below or to the right. Try to keep the statements as short and snappy as you can so they fit easily into the data table and so they have maximum impact. Once again, think of yourself as an advertising headline writer. Go for the most impact with the minimum number of words.

As you enter each comment into the data table, you'll see it appear within its cell and on the edit line near the top of the Data Manager. If the entire comment doesn't fit in the cell when you press Enter, you've got a little bit of adjusting to do. You can widen the columns, increase the heights of the rows, or reduce type size of the text. Widening columns means you can fit more text across each cell. Increasing the heights of the rows means you can fit more than one line of text in each cell. And reducing the size of text lets you fit more words in the same space. Just be sure the type remains large enough to be readable. Remember, viewers might prefer to ignore your work rather than squint at it.

Whichever method you choose, the final table you see on the presentation page shows only the text you actually see in the data table. In other words, if you can't see it in the data table, you won't see it in the chart, either.

Edit line

Two cells merged with the Merge Cells command on the Edit menu

As you enter text into a cell, it appears both in the cell and in the edit line above.

Selected cell

Word-wrapped text within a row that has been made taller.

Entering Text for a Table Chart into the Data Manager

Fitting Text into the Table

To widen a single column of cells, click on the small vertical line between letters at the top of the column and drag to the right. To widen several columns, highlight them by clicking and dragging the cursor across the letters at the tops of the columns. Then, when you widen one highlighted column, they all widen the same amount.

To enlarge rows of cells vertically so they'll each hold several lines of text, follow a similar procedure, clicking on and dragging down the small horizontal lines between numbers at the left end of the rows. As you type text into rows that are now taller, the text will automatically word wrap at the right side of the cell, continuing onto the next line within the cell.

The size of text in the data table is determined by the color scheme applied to the presentation. To override the color scheme's setting, highlight the cells that contain the text you want to change, and then use

Size on the Type menu. You can also use Style on the Type menu to pick a style that has predefined settings for all the commands on the Type menu.

Cut, Copy, and Clear on the Edit menu can help you revise highlighted cells in a table here, just as they did in the previous chapter, when you were making data charts.

Drawing the Table Chart

Finally, when the data table is set, use Draw Chart on the File menu to transform the data table into a table chart. If you need to return to the Data Manager later to revise the content of the chart, click on the table and press Ctrl-D, or select the Text tool and click anywhere on the table chart.

You can also add a title to a chart, but that's done by changing the chart's options, described on the next two pages. ★

Formatting a Table Chart

The final table chart will look exactly like the data table. Same fonts, same colors.

T he operative rule for formatting table charts is that they always come out looking just like their data tables. Changes you make to Type menu settings (text size, font, and formatting), or to Special menu settings (the widths of columns and the heights of rows), affect how the text is arranged both in the data table and in the final table chart. The commands on the Special menu affect more generally how the entire table chart looks.

Other Special Changes

Choosing Color on the Special menu (or pressing F6) summons the Color dialog box, which lets you change the fill color or the text color inside highlighted cells. Select a color from the color palette and then choose either Fill or Text. Then, select Apply to apply the choice you've made. Select OK when you're satisfied with your color changes.

Number, on the Special menu, lets you change the formatting of any numbers in highlighted cells. Number works just as it does when you're setting up a data table for a data chart; the details are covered in Chapter 4.

Highlight the cells to change in a data table before selecting the menu commands to change the format of the cell's contents.

Display, on the Special menu, lets you turn off the display of row titles (the numbers at the left of rows), of column titles (the letters at the top of columns), or of grid lines (the lines that cross the table and delineate cells). Row and column titles don't show up in table charts anyway, but

turning them off makes the data table you're working on look more like the final table chart. It also takes away the ability to select quickly entire rows or columns, though, and to easily resize them, so you may want to leave row and column titles visible.

Cell Margins, also on the Special menu, provides a little white space around the interior edges of cells. The margins push text in, away from the sides of cells. At any time, you can highlight cells and then increase Cell Margins from its default setting of 0.1 inches to a larger value.

Table Chart Options

When you double-click on a table chart, you won't see quite as many options as you will for other Hollywood charts. You can add a title, specify the progressive build for the chart (useful for screen shows), and set whether the chart's cells are transparent (whether any other objects underneath the chart on the page should be visible).

If you call up a chart's options and then add a title by typing it into the available text box, you'll be adding a second object to the Hollywood page (the table itself is the first object). The formatting for the title is set by the presentation's color scheme, but you can override it by selecting the title and then using the commands on the Type menu. You also can move the title independently of the table by clicking on it and dragging. In fact, because the title is a separate object

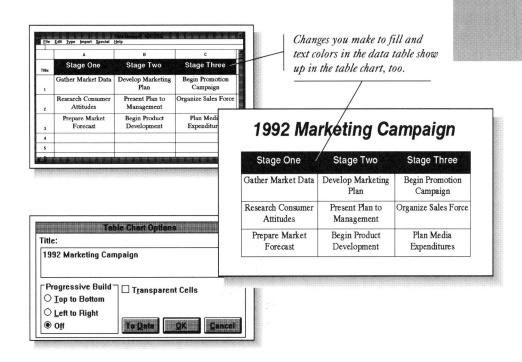

Changes you make to fill and text colors in the data table show up in the table chart, too.

A Data Table and Table Chart Options Combine to Form a Table Chart

(which means you can click on it and select it independently), you can use any of Hollywood's commands to modify it.

In the chapter on Hollywood screen shows, Chapter 9, you'll learn in detail about the progressive build options and how they apply to table charts. ★

Aspects of Table Charts Governed by the Color Scheme

As with most objects you create in Hollywood, some aspects of a table chart's appearance are controlled by options and others are controlled by the color scheme applied to the presentation. Here are the aspects of

table charts that are controlled by the color scheme:

1. Cell Background Color
2. Text Type Style and Color
3. Grid Line Color
4. Title Type Style and Color

Setting Up a Tree Chart

Tree charts, like table charts, are just another kind of text chart. That means you start a tree chart by opening the Text Charts drawer of the Toolbox and selecting the tree chart icon.

Immediately you'll be taken to the Outliner, the same one you learned about in Chapter 3. The difference is that in that chapter, you used the Outliner to organize an entire presentation outline; here, you'll use it to create a miniature outline instead—a tree outline for a single tree chart. In a sense, tree outlines are more like data tables than presentation outlines. Each tree chart has its own tree outline behind it, just as each data or table chart is based on its own data table. So while each presentation can have only one presentation outline, a single presentation may have many tree outlines hiding behind the scenes.

Creating a Tree Outline

To begin setting up a tree, enter at the top of the Outliner the top item in the structure you want to depict (say, the name of the company president, or the chairman of the board of directors). You type it next to the small black circle shown at the top of the window. Then, press Enter to move to the line below. If you want, you can press Shift-Enter; that moves you down a line but without starting a new item, so you can enter more information about the first item — say, the job title below the person's name. Then, as usual, you'd press

Enter to move to the line below.

To enter a list of subordinates, press Tab once to begin indenting the list, or click and hold the mouse button on the circle at the beginning of the new line and drag to the right one indention level. Now, type the list of subordinates, one name under another. To enter a title for each of these, too, press Shift-Enter at the end of each line and type the title on the line below each entry.

At the beginning of any blank line, you can press Tab yet again to move further to the right (down another level in the organizational structure) and type more subordinates.

As you flesh out the tree outline, you can use any of the capabilities of the Outliner that you learned about in Chapter 3. You can collapse and expand portions of the outline by double-clicking on the markers at the beginnings of lines, or you can move an entry and all its subordinates to any point within the outline by simply dragging them. In only a few seconds, you can completely reorganize an organization structure on paper. The real thing might take years to accomplish.

Drawing the Tree

When you've entered an entire structure and you're ready to see the finished tree chart on the current presentation page, use Draw Chart on the File menu. Hollywood asks

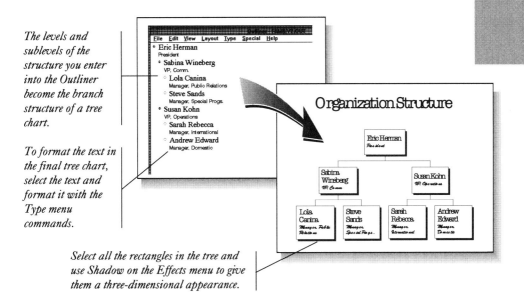

The levels and sublevels of the structure you enter into the Outliner become the branch structure of a tree chart.

To format the text in the final tree chart, select the text and format it with the Type menu commands.

Select all the rectangles in the tree and use Shadow on the Effects menu to give them a three-dimensional appearance.

Using the Outliner to Create a Tree Chart

whether it should save the outline. Select Yes to save the tree outline as a file on disk you can use in another presentation, or select No to go ahead and draw the chart but without saving the outline separately. Even if you select No, the outline is still maintained behind the scenes with the tree chart. It's just not saved on disk as a separate file.

To return to a tree chart's outline, you can always select the chart and then press Ctrl-D or use Data Table/ Outline on the Edit menu. If you double-click on the chart to change its options, selecting To Data on the Options dialog box will also get you back to the chart's outline.

Keep in mind that the tree outline you use to diagram a tree chart is different from a standard presentation

outline, though they are both created in the Outliner. For one thing, the very first line of a presentation outline holds a working title for that outline; it doesn't appear in the presentation. The first line of a tree outline, on the other hand, holds the first level of the tree chart. Obviously, it will appear in the chart. Also, each tree outline holds the information for only one tree chart, while a presentation outline holds the framework for all the charts in the presentation. Also, you get back to the presentation outline by selecting the Bullet Chart tool in the Toolbox or by selecting a page title and pressing Ctrl-D. To get back to a tree outline, you press Ctrl-D after selecting its tree chart. ★

Shaping a Tree Chart

The tree outline you create in the Outliner determines the general shape of your tree chart—the pattern of its branches—but you may want to change the look of some of the tree's leaves or format the text they contain.

You can format leaves and text by following the same convention used throughout Hollywood: select an object first and then use a menu command to format what you've selected, such as centering the text within a leaf. To format several objects simultaneously, press Shift while clicking on those objects; your changes will then apply to them all.

After you select one leaf in a tree chart, you can change its size by stretching it with the mouse. This may reveal more of the text you've got inside, but it also may affect other leaves in the tree. Hollywood strives to maintain an evenly balanced structure. If you make one leaf so large that it would encroach on the space of other leaves, Hollywood may snap it back to a smaller size. You might feel like you're fighting Hollywood rather than controlling it.

A more surefire approach is to change the size of the text in the leaves. Your presentation's overall color scheme sets the default size of text in the tree chart, but you can override this by selecting any of the text and using Size on the Type menu. Of course, you can always use Style to select one of the predefined

combinations of Type menu choices instead.

To select the text in a tree chart's leaves, you can either click on it with the Pointer tool or select the Text tool and wipe across it.

Tree Chart Options

Summoning the options dialog box for the entire tree chart is a little trickier than usual. You need to double-click on the blank space around the tree chart's lines and leaves without clicking on one of them. When you do, you'll see several options. The first lets you enter a title that will span the top of the chart. The title, remember, is an additional text object added above the chart.

The Shape option lets you choose from among five possible shapes for all of the tree's leaves. A sixth option, None, omits the outline of the leaves so that the text floats freely at the ends of the connecting lines. Whatever shape you choose will be the shape of all the tree's leaves. But if you summon the options dialog box by double-clicking on a single leaf, you can select a different shape for just that leaf. The others stay the same.

The Direction option determines

It's better to make the text inside a leaf smaller than to try to increase the size of a leaf.

A tree chart has two sets of options: the options of each line and leaf, and the options of the overall chart.

─────

Shape
- ● Rectangle
- ○ Ellipse
- ○ Rounded Rect.
- ○ Diamond
- ○ Hexagon
- ○ None

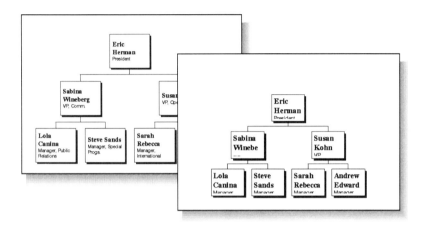

Text in tree charts remains the same size when you resize the chart. You must use the Size command on the Type menu to reduce the text to fit.

the direction of the chart, whether the tree grows from the top, bottom, left,

or right. You can select one of these to flip the chart on its side and create a flow chart from left to right.

Sometimes you'll want the lowest level of subordinates on your chart to be presented as a set of simple lists rather than a row of leaves, each list of names appearing under its superior. The List Last Level option can be turned on at any time to accomplish this.

Double-clicking on one of the lines

in a tree chart leads to another options dialog box, one that shows

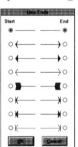

the treatments that are available for either end of that line. The default choice at the top leaves the line as is. The other choices offer a variety of different arrowheads for the starting point and end point of the line. Keep in mind that horizontal lines start at the left and end at the right. Vertical lines start at the top and end at the bottom.

 ★

Where To from Here?

✓ Outlining the Presentation
✓ Adding Bullet and Data
    Charts
✓ Adding Other Chart Types
Next: Adding the Trimmings: Extra
    Text and Graphics
    Formatting the Presentation
    Showing Off Your Work

Your presentation now has all the charts you need. Time to add a few embellishments with Hollywood's Text and Draw tools. The next two chapters cover these in detail.

After these final touches are added, you may want to touch up the overall design with color schemes and templates.

TITLES AND CREDITS

Working with Text

In This Chapter

◆

Formatting the Text in Text Charts

▼

The Text tools can add free-floating text to a page. The Text Charts tools add text charts to pages.

▼

You can use the Text tool to add supplementary text to a text or data chart.

Often it's the little things in life that make all the difference: a small embellishment that adds luster and pizzazz; a bit of information that makes the murky clear.

The principal topic of this chapter is just such a "little thing": an odd line or two of text added to a Hollywood presentation page with the Text tool—text that is on the page, but not part of any chart.

Free-floating text like this can be used in a number of ways. It can label a diagram you've drawn or imported, or it can annotate a graphic data chart. It can compose your presentation's title page, or serve as part of a logo that appears on every page. You can even use it to create full-fledged text charts—say, a bullet chart, with a topic at the top of the page and a list of discussion points below.

But that wouldn't be the most effective use of the Text tool; as you've seen, Hollywood offers a different set of tools, the Text Charts tools, for easily and automatically creating preformatted text charts.

The information you learned in the previous two chapters about how to create bullet charts, table charts, and tree charts is, of course, the meat and potatoes of setting up text charts. But you should also understand the rules that govern how text looks in these charts. The same rules apply to text in data charts, too.

Contradicting the Color Scheme

Every bit of text in a presentation is controlled by the color scheme. The titles of each chart, people's names in a tree chart, the bulleted points in a bullet chart—everything that's text—gets its text font, text size, and other text characteristics from the color scheme. One of the color scheme's principal jobs is to properly format all the text in a presentation according to its design rules.

But you can, if you wish, format the text in text charts independently of the color scheme, overriding the color scheme's control and saying, in effect, "Oh no you don't." The local changes show up in the chart you're working on, but not in any other chart. Notice that you *can* independently change the formatting of the text in text charts, but you *can't* change the formatting of text in data charts without changing the color scheme.

Before you can work on text independently of the color scheme, you must select the text and then make sure that Use Color Scheme under Object Specs on the View menu is turned off. Make sure the box next to Use Color Scheme is unchecked. Hollywood should automatically uncheck Use Color Scheme for each object you try to make an overriding change to, but you may want to inspect it just to be sure. If Use Color Scheme remains checked, the changes you make to the text will disappear the next time you alter the color scheme. The color scheme will simply regain control of the object.

Selecting Text in Text Charts

To select the text in a chart, you need to use an appropriate method for the text chart type. To select all of the text in a *table* chart, click on the table with the Pointer tool. To select just specific text in a table chart, use the Text tool instead, and then click on the table. You'll be transported to the data table in the Data Manager, where you can click on a single cell or wipe across a group of cells that contain the text to format.

To select text to format in a *bullet* chart, click on the text with the Pointer tool. Of course, you'll be able to select either the entire title or the entire group of bulleted text points below. To select an individual text point, you must return to the Outliner and work on the text there.

Select the Text tool rather than the Pointer tool and then click on any text item in the chart. You'll be taken right back to the Outliner. There, click on the marker at the beginning of a line to select an entire topic, or wipe across a single line or even just a portion of a single line to highlight it.

To select text in a *tree* chart, click directly on the text within one of the leaves.

After you've selected the text and made sure Use Color Scheme is off, you can choose any of the commands on the Type menu to alter the appearance of the text. The result of most of these is obvious—Bold makes text bold, Underline underlines, and so on. You'll learn about the more sophisticated Type menu choices when you learn how to format regular text, later in this chapter. ★

Your Map to the Stars

★ You'll learn the difference between the two Text tools (Regular Text & Special Text) on pages 4 and 5.

★ You'll learn how to add regular text and format it with commands on the Type menu on pages 6 through 9.

★ You'll learn how to add and customize special text on pages 10 through 15.

★ You'll learn to use the spell checker and search and replace command on pages 16 and 17.

Regular Text vs. Special Text

W hen you're ready to add a few text objects to a presentation—text that will be separate from any chart that happens to be on the page—you've got two choices: You can add either regular or special text.

You'll find icons for both of these in the Text drawer of the Toolbox. The regular text icon is a large upright letter T, while the special text icon shows a slightly off-kilter T (rotated text is one specialty of special text).

At first, the distinctions between regular and special text seem straightforward. The only possibilities for regular text are those on the Type menu (bold, italic, underline, size, font, etc.), while special text can be stretched, rotated, shadowed, mirrored, and even made to follow a circular path. That sounds as if special text is always preferable. But there are a few considerations you should bear in mind.

Regular Text

First, regular text is governed by the color scheme. Special text is not. To each text object you create with the Regular Text tool, the color scheme gives a *style*—a combination of selections from the Type menu. One style, called "Dutch 24 B," used by bullet chart titles, specifies a 24-point bold Dutch font. Another style you've set up, "Bullets," used on the bulleted points of bullet charts,

specifies an italic, 14-point Swiss font instead. Styles give you the power to quickly select a prepared combination of text attributes.

Special Text

Special text, unlike regular text, is not influenced by the color scheme and you can't use styles to control it. Each special text object gets whatever attributes you select when you add the text. What's more, these attributes don't change, even if you later apply a different color scheme to a presentation or select a different template (which also changes the color scheme). This means you can't use a different color scheme to globally change the format of all the special text in a presentation.

But just as important is that special text isn't produced with ordinary type; it can only be produced from one of the Bitstream font outlines that come with Hollywood. The advantage of outlines is that they describe the shape of characters in the font without limiting them to a specific size. So, after you've added a special text object to a page, you can manually stretch it or shrink it to make it taller and wider, or shorter and thinner. Either way, the general appearance of the characters in the text remains consistent. Only the overall size and shape of the text are distorted.

Special text is more versatile than regular text but it's not subject to control by the color scheme, so you cannot globally reformat it.

Dutch 30 Point Normal

Swiss 42 Point Bold Italic

Swiss 56 Point Outline

Rotated Text

Shadowed Text

Mirrored Text

Circled Text

Regular Text

After you select the Special Text tool, you can draw a rectangle on the screen to specify where the text should fit. That rectangle can be tall and thin or short and squat. That's quite a bit different from using regular text, which limits you to choosing a specific point size for your text from the Type menu.

Hollywood can also perform special feats of daring with the Bitstream outlines that make up special text. It can mirror, shadow, and rotate special

Special Text

text, and make it follow a circular path. Later in this chapter, you'll read about all these special tricks.

The two basic font outlines that come with Hollywood are Swiss (a clean headline font) and Dutch (a more ornate font for body text). For added flexibility, Hollywood comes with several varieties of outline for each font. One of them describes a Swiss bold font. Another describes a Swiss italic font. Another describes a Dutch normal font, and so on. ★

Expanding Your Font Supply

Several fairly recent products can drastically enlarge your stockpile of fonts for Hollywood's regular text. Adobe Type Manager, Bitstream Facelift, and several others are wonderful (and quite inexpensive) little programs; they automatically create characters for Windows programs like Hollywood from a wide variety of typefaces. They display text on the screen in any size, too, just as it will appear when printed.

You must buy these programs separately and install them into Windows, but they'll give you many more fonts than before. What's more, with these programs you can buy most of the popular typefaces and incorporate them into Hollywood.

To increase your selection of fonts for *special* text, you'll need to acquire more Bitstream fonts and install them into Hollywood. The Hollywood manual details this procedure.

Adding and Formatting Regular Text

▼

You can add regular text anywhere on a page and use the Type menu commands to format it.

▼

To change the color of regular text, use Color on the Effects menu.

Adding regular text to a presentation page is simply a matter of selecting the upright T icon in the Text drawer of the Toolbox and then clicking on a page where the text should go. You'll see a text entry box with a blinking, typing cursor (a blinking, vertical bar) positioned inside. Type whatever you want into the box and then click somewhere else on the page to transfer the text to the page. While you're still typing, you can press Enter to move down and add another line.

The text you've just added to the presentation uses the style determined by the color scheme that controls text on the main page. As you'll learn when you learn about color schemes, each page in Hollywood is a main page upon which you place charts.

Each block of text you add with the Text tool is a separate object on the page. That means you can move each block around independently and manipulate it just as you would any other object in Hollywood. For example, you can move a block of text by dragging it to a new location with the mouse, or you can use commands on the Layout menu to reposition it in front of or behind another object you've also placed on the page. When you click on any text you've already added, small handles illuminate to mark a frame

surrounding the text. Dragging these handles changes the shape of the frame, and the text rearranges itself within the frame to fit.

Editing Text on the Main Page

To edit the text in a regular text object, use the Text tool and click where you need a correction made. This moves the typing cursor to that spot. Then, type the correction as though you were working in a word processing program. When you highlight text—by wiping over it with the mouse or by pressing Shift and an arrow key to move the cursor across the text—you can type new text, which instantly replaces whatever is highlighted.

Using the Type Menu

In addition to editing text, you can format it with any of the choices on the Type menu. Whenever you're using the Text tool, you can get to the Type menu quickly just by pressing the right mouse button. To format text, just select the full block of text with the Pointer tool, or use the Text tool to highlight just a segment, and then make selections from the Type menu. These affect only the text you've highlighted.

You should have no trouble recognizing the selections on the Type menu. Most of them are intuitive. **Bold**, *Italic*, <u>Underline</u>, and ALL CAPS do just what you'd think. SMALL CAPS converts highlighted text into all capital letters (with the letters

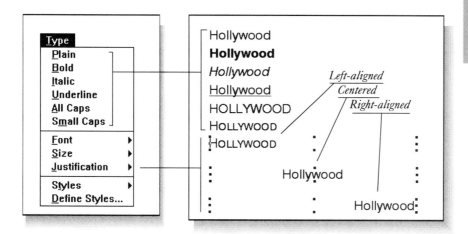

*The Type Menu
Commands*

that were already capitalized now appearing larger than the rest). To remove all of the special Type menu formatting and let the color scheme control the show once again, select Plain.

Three other choices on the Type menu, Font, Size, and Justification, let you choose a typeface for the text, a type size (measured in points: 72 points to an inch), and the text's placement within the text frame (aligned against the left side, aligned against the right side, each line centered, or all lines justified). The Other Size entry box on the Size list is there so you can specify a size that doesn't show up on the list, such as 27 points. The Styles selection on the Type menu lets you choose one of the predefined styles you've already created. Hollywood comes with quite a few of these, but you can add more by following the steps on the next two pages. ★

Now is the time for all good men to come to the aid of their country.

Text word wraps within its frame. Use the frame handles to change the size and shape of a text frame.

Now is the time for all good men to come to the aid of their country.

Setting Up Styles for Regular Text

T he list of styles you get with Hollywood is long indeed, but that doesn't mean you have to be content with it. The styles you get are just a start until you either make your own or customize the ones you already have.

Giving yourself new style choices to work with is easy. You can create a new one (or modify an old one) any time you're working in the main window. The Define Styles command at the bottom of the Type menu pops open a dialog box with five sets of controls: Styles (which lets you choose which style you'll be working on), and four sets of options you can adjust — Font and Size, Attributes, Justification, and Text Spacing. Below the Text Spacing control, the word "Sample" shows you the effect of each adjustment.

To modify an *existing* style, pop down the list under Styles and then double-click on the style name you want. Its current settings will appear in the dialog box, ready for you to change. When you're finished, use Save Style, and presto!, that style now has the new qualities you've chosen for it. To create a *new* style, replace the entry that's currently under Styles with your own. Then change the settings in the dialog box to the ones you want and select Save Style. Your completely new style will be saved under the name you gave it, leaving the original style undisturbed.

Font and Size

The group of controls called Font and Size shows the current typeface (i.e., the font) and current type size for the style name shown at the top. Pull down the Font list to select a different font; pull down the Size list to do the same for size. To choose a size other than those on the Size list, type it into the Other Size: entry box. Type "27" for 27-point type, for example. The Font list will show only those fonts that your output device can produce. Swiss and Dutch are on the list no matter what type of output device you have because they come built into Hollywood.

Attributes and Justification

The Attributes options are self-explanatory. You should note, though, that you can select only those attributes that are available for the font you've selected. A bold outline can't be made italic, for example, so when you select a bold font, the italic attribute is grayed out and unavailable. Justification controls how the text you've selected is aligned within the rectangular frame that surrounds it: either left-aligned, right-aligned, centered, or right- and left-justified.

Text Spacing

The controls in the Text Spacing group let you adjust three things: the amount of horizontal space between characters in the text (printers call

A style is a combination of settings on the Type menu.

Selecting Show in Menu before you save a new style will make the style appear in the list of styles available on the Type menu.

To create a new style, set the controls on this dialog box and then enter a new style name here before selecting Save Style.

When you select any of these attributes, its checkbox will become checked.

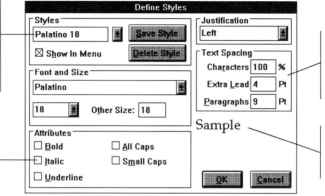

These text-spacing controls let you set extra space between characters, lines, and paragraphs.

This sample shows the effects of the selections you make in this dialog box.

The Define Styles Dialog Box

this letterspacing), the amount of vertical space between successive lines of text (named "lead" after the little chips of lead printers used to insert between lines of metal type), and the additional vertical space above each paragraph of text. To

move characters twice as far apart, for example, set character spacing to 200%. Extra lead (additional space between lines) and paragraph spacing (additional space above each paragraph) are measured in points. ★

Creating Alternate Styles for Bulleted Points

Hollywood has a commitment to consistency. When creating bullet charts, that means the color scheme will apply the same style to every bulleted item in every bullet chart. The result, unfortunately, is that you'll always have the same spacing between lines — regardless of how many bulleted points a particular chart contains. Really, you might prefer to have more space between lines when there are fewer of them and less space between lines when

there are more. One solution is to create several styles (you can name them Close, Medium, and Far) with different settings for extra lead. You'd use Far, which has lots of extra lead, for bullet charts with few bullets, so as to spread them out; and Close, which has little or no extra lead, for bullet charts that have many bulleted lines, in order to fit them all in.

Adding Special Text

Of course, all of the text you write is special. But in Hollywood, some of it is *officially* special: it's added with the Special Text tool. Special text can be

stretched or compressed to any size or shape; it can be rotated, shadowed, mirrored, or bent so that it follows a circular path.

All of these manipulations are possible because special text is based on Bitstream font outlines that Hollywood installs into Windows. A font outline describes the *shapes* of the different characters, but lets Hollywood draw those shapes in any size or position. Bitstream, the maker of these fonts, is a company that designs and sells type for personal computers. The Hollywood installation process installs Bitstream Swiss 721, a clean font without any ornamentation that is especially suitable for chart titles, and Bitstream Dutch 801, a fancier font that is especially appropriate for the main body text of bullet and table charts. For those who know typesetting, Swiss is the Bitstream version of Helvetica and Dutch is the company's version of Times Roman. ITC Zapf Dingbats, a typeface full of little symbols — pointing hands, stars, arrows, and others — is also available for special text.

Adding Special Text

To add special text to the page you're working on, select the special text icon in the Text drawer of the Toolbox. Then, draw a rectangle into which the text should fit. You draw the rectangle by clicking and holding with the mouse at the spot where you want the upper left corner of the rectangle to be, and then dragging the cursor to where the lower right corner should be. When you release the mouse button, the Special Text dialog box appears. Now type your text into the text entry area at the top of the dialog box. Next, select a font for it with the control below. At this point, you *could* also change some of the text's options (you'll learn about these on the next few pages) before selecting OK to place the text on the page—but probably you should place the text on the page first and *then* come back to it and change the options. You'll learn why in the "Sizing Special Text" sidebar on the next page. After the text appears on the page, you can move it with the Pointer tool by dragging it with the mouse to a new position. You also can grab one of the corner or side handles with the mouse and stretch or compress the text. Double-click on the text, and the options dialog box for special text reappears so you can modify the special text options. But that's a topic to take a look at next. ★

▼

Special text will automatically stretch or compress to fit the rectangle you draw for it.

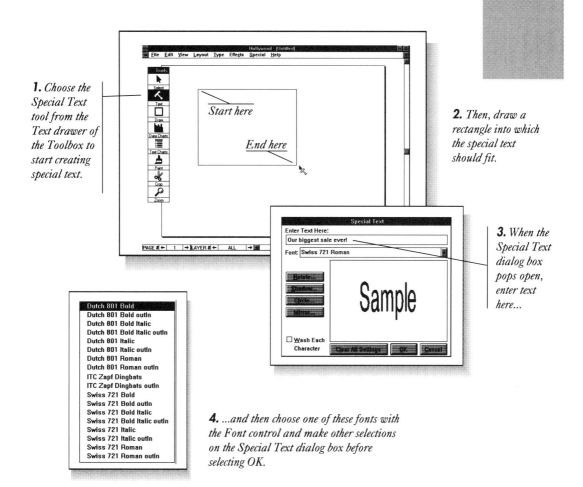

1. Choose the Special Text tool from the Text drawer of the Toolbox to start creating special text.

2. Then, draw a rectangle into which the special text should fit.

3. When the Special Text dialog box pops open, enter text here...

4. ...and then choose one of these fonts with the Font control and make other selections on the Special Text dialog box before selecting OK.

Sizing Special Text

Before you add any of the options for special text, place the text on the page so you can stretch or compress it to fit the space available. *Then* add rotation, a shadow, or any of the other options available in the Special Text dialog box. It's best to do it in that order because after you've added these options, you'll be able

move the text by dragging it, but you won't be able to change its size. If you don't do this little bit of advance work, you'll be frustrated when you must remove all of the enhancements you've applied to the special text before you can change its size by re-sizing the frame that surrounds it.

Rotating, Shadowing, and Circling Special Text

The most special thing about special text is the set of dazzling special effects you can apply to it. Rotating text to any angle, adding a shadow behind it, and shaping it to follow the arc of a circle are sophisticated effects you can apply to special text, but not to regular text. The buttons to select these effects are on the Special Text dialog box you get when you double-click on a special text object. It's the same dialog box you see when you first select the Special Text tool.

Rotating Text

Rotate, the first choice on the Special Text dialog box, in turn calls up a second dialog box that lets you set the degree of rotation of the text (clockwise). A rotation of 90 degrees turns the text completely on its left end, perfect for stretching a word or phrase up the left side of a page—a real "designer" look.

Rotated text can be combined with some other special text options, but not all. It can have a shadow and it can be mirrored, but it can't be circular. You can have as many special text objects on the screen as you want, and each can have a different angle of rotation.

Shadowing Text

Adding shadows can give special text a stylish and very impressive three-dimensional effect. The Shadow option calls up a second dialog box that shows a shadow behind the letter "T." The dialog box has scroll bars you can use to adjust the depth of the shadow in two directions. If you prefer, you can type in exact horizontal and vertical measurements for the shadow instead, especially if you want to specify the exact same degree of

You can select any of the special text options when you enter text into the Special Text dialog box or afterwards, when you double-click on special text you've already created.

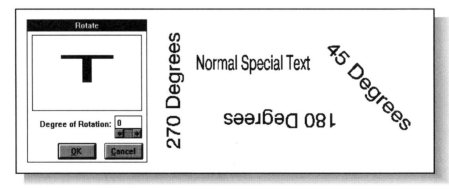

Rotating Special Text

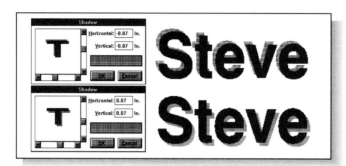

Shadowing Special Text

shadow on several text objects. Using the scroll bars is quick and easy, though, and it gives you a good sense of what the final text will look like.

The rectangle to the right of the sample shadow is filled with the same color as the shadow. Double-click on it to call up the color palette and select a different color. Usually, a dark shadow behind light-colored text works well.

Circling Text

Bending text into an arc, the intent of the Circle option, can be helpful for creating special logos or graphic designs. The choices for the circle option let you run text around the inside of a circle at its top or bottom. The Inside Percentage control determines the height of the text inside the imaginary circle.

Circular text lacks a bit of flexibility, though. It appears on the page wherever you drew the box when you started to add special text. To change the radius of the circle around which the text flows, you can click on the circular text object and drag a corner handle in or out, but then the height of the text characters changes proportionally. Try it and you'll see that you can't make the circle bigger without making the text larger, too. ★

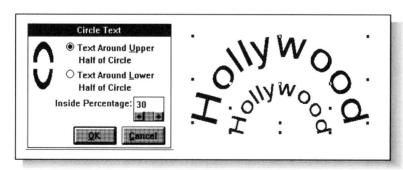

Circling Special Text

Mirroring and Washing Special Text

Mirroring special text either turns it upside down or flips it left side for right—as though you were looking at it in a mirror. You may not need to demonstrate such a thing often, but you may want to use it to create special effects for logos or for interesting graphic designs. The Mirror dialog box shows the result of each mirror effect. Show Original and Mirror Text, at the top of the Mirror dialog box, shows the original text opposite the mirrored text.

Applying a Color Wash

A color wash is a gradual transition across an area from one color to another, or even from one color to a second color to still a third. One color wash might go gradually from light blue to dark blue. Another might go from yellow to orange to dark red, like a sunset.

Color washes can be stunning when used as the background of a presentation. And they can also be flashy inside objects you place on Hollywood pages, including inside special text.

Special text that has a color wash starts with one color at one end of the block of text and ends with another color at the other end. If you turn on Wash Each Character in the Special Text dialog box, each character gets its own color wash instead, graduating from one color at the top of a character to another at the bottom, or graduating from left to right within each character.

The direction of the transition within special text depends on the direction of the color wash chosen.

▼

You can use as many different color washes in as many different special text objects as you want.

▼

Make sure the special text you've created is sized properly before you try to apply special effects to it.

Hollywood (Original Special Text)

Mirror Set to Top

Hollywood (Original)

Mirror Set to Bottom

Hollywood (Original)

Mirror Set to Left

booʍʅʅoH Hollywood (Original)

Mirror Set to Right

(Original) HollywoodbooʍʅʅoH

*Color Wash from
Left to Right*

Hollywood

*Color Wash from
Upper Left to
Lower Right with
Wash Each
Character On*

Hollywood

*Radial Color Wash
(center out)*

Hollywood

You'll learn how to set up your own color wash that comes with Hollywood or one you've designed yourself by selecting the text and then selecting Color Wash on the Effects menu (pressing the right mouse button pops open the Effects menu the fastest). The Color Wash dialog box lists all of the color washes currently available, and it lets you design your own.

Radial color washes, those that change color from the center out rather than across an object, are centered in the middle of a block of special text or in the middle of each special text character. Using Radial washes can slow down Hollywood considerably as they take a long time for the program to calculate. Adding radial color washes when everything else is finished is the best idea.

Clearing All Settings

The Clear All Settings button on the Special Text dialog box returns special text to its generic state, without any special effects. You'll need to clear all of the special effects at once if what you want to do is stretch or compress special text you've already created. To be a little less dramatic about it, you can reduce the degree of special text effects to zero selectively, which means you can clear certain settings rather than having to clear all of them at once. ★

Using Spell Check and Search+Replace

Even if you once won every spelling bee in the state of Kansas, you still should use Hollywood's built-in spell checker to verify the accuracy of your text. Minor typos loom large when they're projected in front of an audience.

The spell checker compares every word in your presentation with the words in its own dictionaries. Should it not find a match—a misspelling or a proper name, perhaps—the spell checker suggests a correction and makes it, if you wish. Now, don't think running a presentation through the spell checker can replace giving it a good hard read before showing it to someone. The spell checker can catch straightforward typos, such as "benifits" when you meant "benefits," but it can't tell when words are missing, it doesn't know that a word should be plural rather than singular, and it won't tell you to use "they're" rather than "their" or "there." You can spell check the presentation outline, but it's better to check the individual presentation pages instead, because then Hollywood checks the titles and footnotes of data charts and all the text in table and tree charts. Hollywood never checks special text, though, nor the data, labels, and legends of data charts.

Spell Checking

To use the spell checker, move the cursor to the top of the first page of the presentation or to the top of the

presentation outline, and then use Check Spelling on the Special menu.

In a moment, you'll see the Check Spelling dialog box. The current entry below Main Dictionary, US, is the standard Hollywood dictionary. If you use IBM DisplayWrite and have a foreign-language dictionary, you can enter the dictionary name here as a replacement to the standard US English dictionary.

If you've never used the spell checker before, the entry below User Dictionary will be blank. The user dictionary is a supplementary dictionary that Hollywood also checks when it's trying to find a match for the words in your presentation. Into the user dictionary, you can add names and terms that aren't in the main dictionary but that you tend to use frequently, so Hollywood will find them when it checks a presentation. If a user dictionary has been set up by someone else, you should see its name in the User Dictionary box. If the box is blank, you should enter a name for your own user dictionary.

Then, to begin the actual spell check, select Start. If no unknown words are found, Hollywood tells you "Spelling Check Completed." If it finds words that are not in the main or user dictionary, Hollywood opens a second window above the first; there,

---

You're better off spell checking individual pages rather than the presentation outline so that Hollywood checks the text in charts, too.

Don't rely on the spell checker to catch every mistake. It can't know if words are missing, among other things.

it indicates the unknown word and offers a list of alternatives, underneath Suggestions. Either select one of the suggested words or type the correction into the box below Change To:. Then, select Change. If the unknown word is one you'd like to add to your user dictionary, select Add instead. If the word is not in the dictionary but it's acceptable as is, select Ignore. The spell checker works its way through the presentation until it finishes the last page, and then tells you it's done.

Searching and Replacing

Search+Replace, also on the Special menu, lets you search for words in a presentation and then, if you want, replace them with other words.

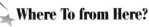

To search for a word, move the cursor to the top of the first page in the presentation, or else to the top of the outline, and then select Search+Replace on the Special menu. In the box below Search For:, type the words you want to locate. To replace those words with others, type the replacement words in the box below Replace With:. Then, select Search to search for a word, Replace to substitute the replacement word for the word found, or Change All to search and replace throughout the entire presentation or outline. To search only for complete words that match the search word exactly, select Whole Word. Or, to find any word that contains the letters of the search word (for example "*the*ater" because it contains the search word "the"), select Partial Word. To disregard capitalization (letting you find "us" even though the search word is "US"), select Ignore Case. To search only for words with the identical capitalization, select Case Sensitive instead. You probably won't need to bother with these settings to perform a successful search. When Hollywood reaches the end of your document, it proudly declares, "Search+Replace Completed!" ★

Where To from Here?

✓ Outlining the Presentation
✓ Adding Bullet and Data Charts
✓ Adding Other Chart Types
Next: Adding the Trimmings: Extra Text and Graphics
Formatting the Presentation
Showing Off Your Work

You've added free-floating regular and special text to your presentation to annotate its pages. Now is the time to add graphic touches with Hollywood's Draw tools. You'll learn that you can also use the Draw tools to create illustrations from scratch. But that's the subject of the next chapter.

IMAGE MAKING

Drawing in Hollywood

In This Chapter

◆

Working with Objects

▼

Look in the
drawer of the
Toolbox labeled
"Draw" to find all
the basic shapes
you need.

▼

Each shape you
draw, even with
the Paintbrush
and Spray Can
tools, is a
separate object.
Its options set
many aspects of
its appearance.

L ike every great movie studio, Hollywood has an "art department" fully equipped with drawing tools to delight any artist. Along with the tools comes an assortment of ready-made shapes, patterns, lines, and colors that artists can use to conjure up images.

You're not an artist? Well, that doesn't mean you can't use Hollywood's drawing tools in your own way: say, to spruce up a cut-and-dried presentation with a background pattern, a color wash, and maybe another artistic flourish or two.

Oh, you even flunked finger painting? Well then, you'll be happy to know that Hollywood comes with dozens of already-drawn pictures that you can simply drop into your presentations. There's a map of the United States, for example, that you could use in a talk about U.S. marketing efforts; or a bull's-eye for a spiel about how your new promotional campaign is "right on target." For this, you need only enough artistic sense to judge where one of Hollywood's pictures should go.

However you use Hollywood's drawing and editing tools — to create original art or simply to touch up presentation pages — you should first understand a few basic concepts about drawing in Hollywood.

The Draw Drawer

The drawer of the Toolbox labeled "Draw" is where you're most likely to start when you're ready to draw in Hollywood. Open the drawer and you'll find six basic tools for adding six basic shapes to pages. Another drawer (labeled "Paint") holds two other related tools, the Paintbrush and the Spray Can; one lets you draw freehand on the surface of a page, while with the other you can spray a mist of dots on the page, just as you would with a real-life can of spray paint.

Objects Are the Subject

Each individual shape you add to a page is a separate object. As you've learned, options are what refine the appearance of an object. The same holds true here.

In this chapter, you'll learn how to add each object and set its options to give it the best possible look. You'll also find out, among other things, how to resize objects, move them, and change their order when they overlap.

In addition to the tools that let you add objects, you'll learn about commands on the Edit, View, Layout, and Special menus that help you refine objects, zoom in to work on them in detail, position objects precisely, and change their basic color or design.

All the ways you can create and modify graphic objects make Hollywood a very powerful canvas on which to compose. But Hollywood is far more powerful than any traditional canvas could ever be — for reasons you're about to learn.

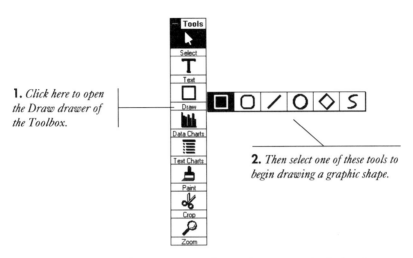

1. *Click here to open the Draw drawer of the Toolbox.*

2. *Then select one of these tools to begin drawing a graphic shape.*

Multiple Objects and Multiple Layers

With Hollywood, you can group several objects into a single object. Manipulating that one combined object now affects all of the objects in the group. It's nice to know, for example, that after you've carefully combined several objects to construct a handsome company logo, by grouping them you can transform them into a single object for easy moving and resizing.

Hollywood's Layers, another key capability, are like transparent overlays placed on top of the base presentation page. You can draw on any layer, or move objects to various layers, and then you can reveal or conceal specific layers to call attention to particular aspects of the drawing

Layers are also an integral part of the animated presentations called screen shows, which — as if you haven't guessed — you can show on the screen. Screen shows build pages one layer at a time. Instruct Hollywood to automatically break a chart apart onto separate layers, and you can then see it reassembled later as part of a screen presentation.

The Master Page

One of the most important elements of Hollywood drawing is the Master Page. Place an object on the Master Page, and it shows up at the same spot on every page in the presentation. Using the Master Page can save you the work of copying onto every page some graphic object that you want repeated throughout the presentation. You might use the Master Page to place the same graphic symbol on the right side of every page, or perhaps to place the company mascot in the background of every slide in a slide show.

In the rest of this chapter, you'll learn how to use all of Hollywood's drawing and image manipulation capabilities. You'll find good, creative uses for them every time you start up Hollywood. ★

Draw Objects I: Boxes and Circles

When you're ready to investigate the shapes you can add to Hollywood pages, take a look at boxes and circles first: they're easy to add, and they're representative of all the other shapes you can use. Creating other Hollywood shapes employs the same general procedures.

Drawing Boxes

The Box tool in the Draw drawer of the Toolbox lets you draw both rectangles and squares. After you've  selected the Box tool (it's the first tool on the left), move the cursor back to the page, put it at one corner of the rectangle or square you imagine, and then press and hold the mouse button. Drag the cursor diagonally across where you want the rectangle or square to be, from one imaginary corner to its opposite, and then release the mouse button. You've got your box! To form a perfect square, hold down the Shift key while dragging the cursor. The color scheme determines the color and fill pattern you get inside the box.

You don't have to be satisfied with where you've placed an object, of course. To move it, click somewhere within its interior, hold the mouse button down, and then drag it to a new position. To change its size or shape, click on it and then drag to a new position one of the small handles that surround it. Moving and resizing

any object in Hollywood works the same way.

Box Options

Clicking on an object once selects it. Double-clicking on an object produces something different altogether. A dialog box appears showing its current options: in the case of boxes, the settings for Chisel Effect and 3D Effect.

Chisel Effect adds beveled edges to a box, making it look as though it's raised off the page. Use the Amount of Effect control to increase the width of the chiseled edge. You'll see how your changes look on the sample square in the dialog box.

The small buttons surrounding the sample square determine where light appears to be coming from and how shadows fall on the box. Click on the button in the upper left corner, for example, and light illuminates the Chisel Effect from the upper left.

3D Effect gives boxes sides that extend into the distance. Use the scroll bars beside the sample square on the right to control the depth of the sides and the direction they extend. You can also type in exact measurements just below the sample square — a useful method for applying to one box the same amount of 3D effect you've used on another one.

For extra pizzazz, you can use both Chisel Effect and 3D Effect at the same time, adding a beveled edge to a three-dimensional box.

▼

A box is defined by two points at its opposite corners.

▼

You draw a box to specify the boundaries of a circle, too.

116

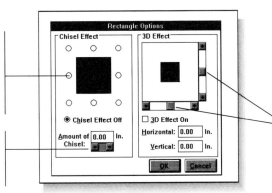

Click on one of these eight buttons to set the direction of the pseudo light source.

Use this control to set the depth of the chisel effect.

Use these scroll bars to control the depth and direction of the 3D effect.

Drawing Rounded Boxes

The rounded box tool in the Draw drawer, just to the right of the normal box tool, lets you draw rectangles and

squares that have rounded corners. You add a rounded box just as you would a normal box. But then, when you double-click on it, a scroll bar appears in the options dialog box that lets you change the degree of rounding. A box with zero rounding is a rectangle. One with a rounding of 99 is very close to a circle.

Drawing Circles and Ellipses

Drawing circles and ellipses is much like drawing squares and rectangles. You select the Circle tool from the Toolbox, then position the cursor at one corner of an imaginary

box that would delineate the size of the circle you want. Hold the mouse button and move the cursor to the diagonally opposite corner of the rectangle. If you press and hold Shift while you move the cursor, when you release the mouse button you'll get a perfect circle rather than an ellipse.

Unlike boxes, circles have no options. Go ahead: double-click on a circle you've drawn and Hollywood will tell you so. ★

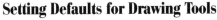

Setting Defaults for Drawing Tools

When you hold down the Ctrl key while selecting a tool from the Toolbox, the default options for that tool appear in a dialog box. The default options are those the tool applies to objects when it draws them. You can override the default options by double-clicking on the object after it's drawn and changing its options manually.

Setting new defaults comes in handy when you want to draw a whole bunch of objects with the same specifications. Just change the default options until you've added all of the objects, and then reset the defaults to their original status.

Draw Objects II: Lines, Polygons, & Polylines

D rawing lines is particularly easy. After you select the Line tool from the Toolbox, click on where the starting end of the line should be, and then hold the mouse button down until you've

dragged the cursor to the ending end. The line that forms when you release the mouse button will have three handles. Drag the middle handle to move the entire line to another position. Use one of the end handles to move just that end. If you have trouble selecting a thin line so its handles appear, draw a box around the entire line with the Pointer tool to select it.

Double-clicking on a line shows a wide variety of line endings for both the starting and ending ends of the line. Now choose one of the arrowheads. Should an arrowhead you choose refuse to appear on your line, you'll need to check Lines on the Effects menu: make sure a choice other than None is selected.

When your line first appears on the page, it will be in the style established by the color scheme. You can always choose a different style from the Effects menu. You'll learn about that later in this chapter.

Adding Polygons

No doubt you'll remember from high school that a polygon is "a closed plane figure bounded by straight

lines." Or maybe you won't. Either way, the polygon tool in the Toolbox looks like a diamond; that's because, at first, the polygons you draw will be diamond shaped. You can change their shape after you've got them on the page: by double-clicking on them, you'll get to see several possible polygon styles.

Regular polygons, the default, are symmetrical. Hollywood draws them for you with sides of equal lengths. To change the number of sides to your polygon, enter the new number of sides in the Polygons & Polylines options dialog box.

Irregular polygons, on the other hand, are composed of a number of connected line segments you draw yourself. The first and last line segments you draw are then connected, as explained below, to form a closed object that's filled with a color and pattern.

Poly*lines* are nothing more than a series of these line segments, connected one to the next but not with the first and last lines joined. In other words, a polyline is an open-ended shape.

The best way to start a polygon or polyline is to hold down the Ctrl key while selecting the Polygon tool; this lets you select a polygon style from the Polygons & Polylines options dialog box before you start. To create

▼

Hold down the Ctrl key when you select the Polygon tool to choose a polygon style before you draw it.

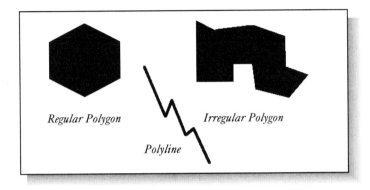

Regular Polygon

Irregular Polygon

Polyline

Polygon Styles

a regular polygon, first select Regular Polygons, then choose how many sides it will have, and then draw a rectangle on the page to contain your polygon. As you finish drawing the rectangle, a polygon appears in its place.

To create an irregular polygon, select Ctrl when you select the Polygon tool and then select Irregular from the options dialog box. Now draw a series of line segments. It's easy; here's how: First draw a single line. Now click elsewhere on the page. Each time you click, Hollywood extends a new line from the previous one to meet the new click point. Double-click at the last point to finish the polygon.

To draw a polyline, follow the same operations but first select Polyline from the options dialog box. If your polyline accidentally comes out filled, as if it were a polygon, make sure Fills on the Effects menu is set to None.

Moving the Points of Polygons or Polylines

You can change the overall size of a polygon by selecting it and then dragging the handles of the box that surrounds it. But if you want to move the individual points of a polygon or polyline, or change its shape, you must use Edit Polygon on the Edit menu after selecting the object. You'll see a small box appear at each point along the polygon or polyline. Position the cursor on one of these boxes (the cursor changes to a box shape, too) and then click and drag the box, and the point along with it, to a new location.

To add or delete points, double-click on one of the small boxes. The line segment that begins at that point will become highlighted, and the Poly Points Edit dialog box appears. Now select Add Points on the dialog box to add new points along the highlighted line segment (enter the appropriate number of points in the dialog box), or select Delete Point to delete the point you've selected.

When you're finished, you must select the Pointer tool again to continue doing other things in Hollywood. Try pressing the right mouse button and you'll see the easiest way to get back to the Pointer tool. ★

Draw Objects III: Bezier Curves

Bezier curves are curving lines that have a control point at each place where the curve changes direction. Each control point can be moved, and you can change the shape of a curve very precisely by adjusting the angle at which the curve approaches each point. Bezier curves are an alternative to curves you might draw freehand with the Paintbrush tool. But Bezier curves are guaranteed to curve smoothly, and the path they follow can be modified. Curves drawn with the Paintbrush can only be moved or resized.

The way to draw a Bezier curve is to select the Bezier tool from the Draw drawer of the Toolbox and then click on the screen where the curve should begin. Now, start drawing your line by moving the cursor to another point along the path of the curve you've imagined, and clicking and holding the mouse button while dragging the cursor a little way in the direction the curve should continue.

You'll get a control point where you first clicked. Then, position the cursor on the next point the curve should continue through, and click and drag again in the direction the curve should move off in from there. Continue until you've created all of the segments of the curve. Don't be discouraged if the curve seems to go the wrong way at first. Drawing Bezier curves properly takes some practice. Just remember that at each new point, you should drag the cursor a little to indicate in which direction the curve should now continue.

Adjusting the Bezier Curve

To move a Bezier curve or change its overall size, you can click anywhere along the curve and then drag the handles of the box that surrounds it. But to edit the actual shape of the curve, select the Pointer tool, click somewhere along the curve, and then use Edit Bezier on the Edit menu. You'll see the control

The Bezier Curve tool is useful for drawing smooth curves that you can adjust very precisely.

To draw a curve by hand instead, use the Paintbrush tool.

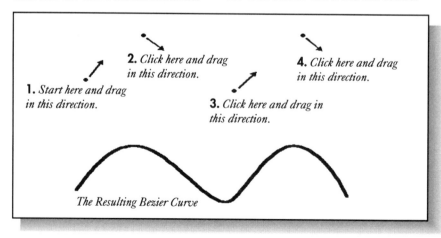

2. *Click here and drag in this direction.*

4. *Click here and drag in this direction.*

1. *Start here and drag in this direction.*

3. *Click here and drag in this direction.*

The Resulting Bezier Curve

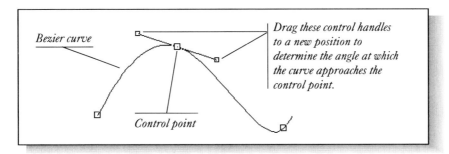

Bezier curve

Drag these control handles to a new position to determine the angle at which the curve approaches the control point.

Control point

Editing a Bezier Curve

points for the curve reappear so you can manipulate the curve with them.

Click on any control point and drag it to a new position to move a part of the curve. To change the angle at which the curve approaches a point, click and drag one of the pair of control handles that stick out from the point. Try clicking on the far end of the control handle (farthest from the control point) and dragging it away from the point to lengthen the handle. Or try moving the control handle so it extends in a different direction from the point, thereby changing the line's angle of attack toward the point.

Editing Bezier Curve Points

Double-clicking on any control point along a Bezier curve highlights the segment of the curve that begins at the point and summons the Edit Bezier Point dialog box so you can add or delete points, break the curve at one of the points, or change that segment of the curve to a straight line.

Add Point to Curve, in the dialog box, adds another point at the middle

of the highlighted curve segment. Break Curve breaks the Bezier curve right at the selected control point. Now you've got two curves you can drag apart. Delete Curve removes the highlighted segment altogether.

If you double-click on either the first or last point of a Bezier curve, you'll see another option, Join Curve, which joins the first and last points of the curve to form a single, unbroken curving line.

The four buttons at the top of the dialog box are important, too. Selecting Line turns the highlighted segment into a straight line, while Curve turns a straightened segment back into a curve. Smooth causes the pair of control handles sticking out of a point to work in tandem. Move one and the other moves, too, so the curve remains smooth as it passes through the point. Sharp lets you move the control handles independently so you can change the direction of the curve sharply as it passes through the point.

When you're finished editing a Bezier curve, you'll need to select the Pointer tool so you can do other things in Hollywood. ★

Using the Paintbrush and the Spray Can

Two of Hollywood's most fun tools are the Paintbrush and the Spray Can. Both of these tools are in the Toolbox drawer labeled "Paint," and are just like their real-life counterparts. The Paintbrush tool lets you paint on the page like Picasso, while the Spray Can tool lets you spray across the page like a graffiti artist.

Fill lets you change the color of the paint on the paintbrush, but it's inactive when you're setting default options. You'll need to go back and double-click on something you've already painted to change its color or fill pattern. The color Hollywood uses on its own is controlled by the color scheme setting that governs the look of objects drawn on the main page.

Paintbrush Options

As with other drawing tools, you can hold down the Ctrl key while selecting Paintbrush or Spray Can to set its default options. These will remain until you change them again. If you hold down Ctrl while selecting the Paintbrush tool, you'll see three options: Size, Color/Fill, and Shape. Using the scroll bars to change Size lets you modify the width of the brush you choose from the collection below, next to Shape. The dialog box shows the appearance of the brush as you make changes. Normally, Color/

Spray Can Options

When you hold down the Ctrl key while selecting the Spray Can tool, you'll see similar options to those you see when you use the Paintbrush tool, except that Shape has been replaced with Flow Rate, which determines the density of the spray — how close together the little dots of color are packed. By dragging the scroll bar next to this control, you can adjust the Flow Rate from 0 (no flow) to 10 (maximum flow).

Objects drawn with the Spray Can tool do not maintain their appearance

After you've draw a freehand line with the Paintbrush tool, you can use Color on the Effects menu to change its color.

Hollywood is not capable of printing objects you've drawn with the Spray Can tool. Use this tool for adding sprayed areas for screen shows only.

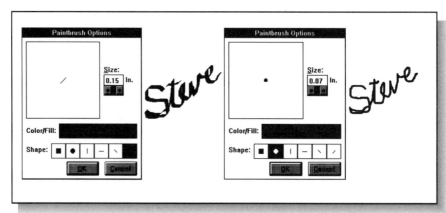

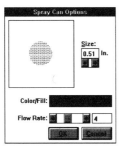

Using the Spray Can Tool

well when you change their size. When you stretch a sprayed object, its dots become larger and more spread out, so the sprayed area looks less dense. Instead, you may decide to delete the sprayed object and then respray a new one of the correct size in order to maintain the same density of dots you had before.

Crop Tool

The Crop tool lets you select a rectangular portion of a graphic file to display. The rest of the image remains in the file, but it does not appear on the Hollywood screen.

You can use the Crop tool only with bit-mapped images (.TIF, .PCX, and

.BMP are three bit-mapped file formats Hollywood can import). It doesn't work with Hollywood's clip art.

To use the Crop tool, import a bit-mapped image onto a page using Import Picture on the File menu. Then, select the Crop tool and click on the image. With the Crop tool, you can drag the image's frame handles in toward the middle of the image until the frame surrounds only the portion of the image you want to display. Now, you can use the Pointer tool to resize the image just as you would any object. ★

Before and After Using the Crop Tool

Special Screen Controls

Set the measurement scale of the ruler when you set up the preference file.

The coordinates and Snap to Grid can help you align objects. You can also use Align on the Layout menu to align objects you've already drawn.

Eyeballing the placement of objects may set your creativity free when you're using Hollywood to create original art. But sometimes you want a little more precision in positioning objects, so Hollywood's Layout menu offers several screen aids with which you can work.

The rulers runs across the top of the main presentation window and down its left side, marking off distances across the page. The grid superimposes on the page small dots at a fixed spacing. You can use these dots to gauge distances and align objects, or you can make the cursor snap to them, automatically jumping to the nearest dot as you draw. Hollywood's coordinates let you see exactly how far the cursor has traveled as you draw.

The Magnifying Glass, a tool in the Toolbox, lets you zoom in on any rectangular portion of the presentation window for close-in, detailed work on a page.

The Ruler

When you use Show Ruler, on the Layout menu, you'll see sliding markers within the rulers; they move as the cursor moves. These markers can help you accurately position the cursor as you use any of Hollywood's drawing tools.

When you first select Show Ruler, both the horizontal and vertical rulers will have their zero points set at the upper left corner of the presentation

window, where the two rulers meet. To designate a new zero point, click somewhere along the length of either ruler. To zero the rulers more precisely, click and hold down the mouse button on the small rectangle in the upper left corner of the screen, where the horizontal and vertical rulers meet. Then, drag the cursor onto the screen and to the new zero point you'd like. To reset the zero point of both rulers back to the upper left corner of the page, double-click on that same small rectangle in the upper left corner.

To change the measurement scale used by the ruler (inches, centimeters, points, or picas), you'll need to change the measurement system in the presentation's preferences. You'll learn about preferences in Chapter 8.

Coordinates

Coordinate numbers, when they're on, show up in a small box next to the cursor as it moves across the screen. They tell the horizontal (X) and vertical (Y) distance the cursor has moved since starting a drawing command. To see coordinates, use Show Coordinates on the Layout menu. Coordinates can be helpful when you want to draw an object of a very specific size.

The Grid

The grid, a series of evenly spaced dots on the screen, is controlled by commands on the Layout menu. Of course, these dots don't show up in

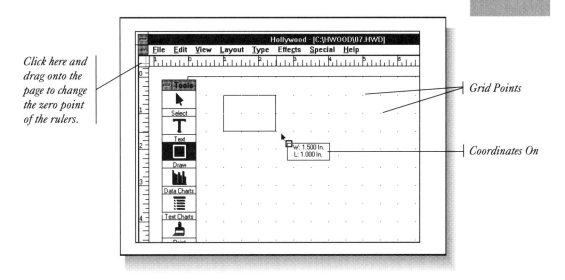

Click here and drag onto the page to change the zero point of the rulers.

Grid Points

Coordinates On

Hollywood's Screen Controls

the final presentation; they're just around to help you position the cursor. What makes the grid especially helpful is that you can force the cursor to snap to the nearest grid point when you draw an object. To draw a design with objects that are spaced evenly one inch apart, you can use the grid to jump the cursor neatly to those positions.

Show Grid, on the Layout menu, does just what you'd think. When the grid is on, Hide Grid on the Layout menu makes it disappear, although its effects are still felt if you have Snap to Grid on. Pressing F4 repeatedly toggles Snap to Grid on and off. Layout Grid (F3) lets you specify the horizontal and vertical spacing of the dots. When Grid in Back is checked,

the grid shows up behind objects you've placed on the screen. Otherwise, it is superimposed over the objects.

The Magnifying Glass Tool

The Magnifying Glass tool, in its own drawer of the Toolbox labeled "Zoom," lets you draw a rectangle around a portion of the presentation page you'd like to examine a little closer. After you've zoomed in, you can continue to use all of Hollywood's tools. To zoom back out, you must use the commands on the View menu (Zoom Out, which is the opposite of Zoom In, or Size to Fit, which changes the view so you can see the entire page on the screen). ★

Overlapping, Aligning, and Grouping Objects

A s you work to perfect an image composed of several objects, you may find that the objects overlap, but not in the order you intended. Objects you need to see are hidden, partly or completely, behind others. Hollywood provides a set of commands on the Layout menu to rectify this problem and others.

Send to Back and Bring to Front shuffle whatever object or objects you've highlighted, bringing them to the top of a stack of objects or pushing them to the bottom. Nudge Forward and Nudge Backward are a little more subtle. They move objects one layer forward or back. An object that sits atop two others, for example, moves back between the others when you select it and use Nudge Backward.

Alignment

Alignment, also on the Layout menu, lines up objects with one another or with a specified part of the page. Vertical alignment (a choice you'll see in the Alignment dialog box when you follow the instructions below) moves the objects in a selected group up or down so that all their tops, middles, or bottoms are lined up, and Horizontal alignment moves selected objects left or right so that all their left sides, middles, or right sides are lined up. Choosing Top for Vertical alignment, for example, moves all selected objects so that

their tops are lined up with the top of the highest selected object. Choosing the same option with Align To Page already selected moves all selected objects so that they are up against the top of the page.

To use Alignment, you must select more than one object, either by holding down Shift as you click on the objects or by drawing a box around them with the Pointer tool. The box must completely enclose the objects you want selected, and only those objects. Other objects enclosed in the box will be included, too, whether you want them or not. Beware also that if a part of an object sticks outside the box, it won't be selected.

When you use Alignment on the Layout menu — the next step after selecting your objects — a dialog box appears with a number of options. A sample of three objects shows you how the current selection in the dialog box will affect the arrangement of your objects. You'll want to examine the sample carefully before selecting OK to actually carry through the Alignment options: once made, alignment changes can't be undone.

Grouping

By using the Group command, you can combine several objects into one object, either permanently or just temporarily. Any changes to a grouped object will affect all of its

---

You can use Align on text as well as on graphic objects. It can help you left-align several lines of text under one another.

Use Group to combine several related objects into a single object for easy editing and repositioning

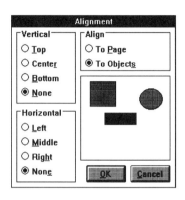

The Alignment Dialog Box

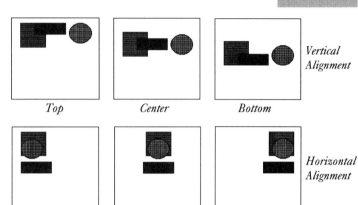

Vertical Alignment

Top   *Center*   *Bottom*

Horizontal Alignment

Left   *Middle*   *Right*

component objects, too. Grouping is particularly helpful when you've added to a page a number of objects that together form a single design. By grouping the objects, you can easily move the entire design from place to

Maple Leaf Syrup

Three Objects Grouped into a Single Object

place, or make any other editing changes Hollywood allows. For example, using Color on the Effects menu to select a color for the group changes all the objects in the group to that color.

To group objects, select them first, either by holding the Shift key while you click on each or by containing them in a box with the Pointer tool.

Then, use Group on the Edit menu, or press F2 (the quickest way). Now, you'll find that you simply can't select a single object without selecting the whole group. Ungroup, or pressing Alt-F2, breaks apart into its components a group you've selected. Obviously this applies only to sets of objects you've already turned into a group.

Layers

Another set of commands on the Layout menu controls Hollywood's layers — transparent overlays you can place on a background page. Layers let you break a drawing apart, placing different objects onto various overlays so that you can reveal parts of the drawing selectively. You'll learn about layers in detail in Chapter 9, which covers screen shows. Using layers properly is integral to setting up a screen show. ★

Applying Effects with the Effects Menu

▼

Commands on the Effects menu override the color scheme. To let the color scheme take control of an object once again, select the object, select Object Specs on the View menu, and then select Use Color Scheme. Make sure the box next to Use Color Scheme is checked.

The look of an object is determined in a number of ways. Some aspects of its appearance are directed by options, which you summon by double-clicking on the object. Others are governed by your presentation's color scheme. But the controls on the Effects menu are important, too. So important, in fact, that although Effects is on the Hollywood main menu, you can always jump to it instantly by pressing the right button of the mouse.

Some of the commands on the Effects menu override the color scheme's control over objects. That's probably just what you want. Just realize that, should you want to make the same change to all objects in the presentation, it would be better to change the color scheme instead.

Changing Fill Patterns

The pattern that fills an object is called its fill. After you select an object, you can use Fill on the Effects menu to change the pattern that fills the object. When you select Fill, a secondary menu opens with nine standard fill patterns, plus None (hollow) and Solid (a solid color without a pattern). Custom..., also on this secondary menu, lets you design and save your own fill patterns and then decide which should appear on the Fill menu. Once you've chosen a fill pattern from this secondary menu you see when you select Fills, that pattern goes into all the objects you have selected.

Changing Line Styles

The lines you've drawn can be modified, too, using either line styles that come with Hollywood or styles you create yourself. The styles differ from one another in thickness and color.

After you select a line to modify and then use Lines on the Effects menu, you'll see a secondary menu that displays several line styles you can choose among. It also displays an option called Custom... that lets you design your own.

The Custom Lines dialog box lets you set up a special line that is actually made up of three stripes side by side. Each stripe of this three-part line can be set for its own color and thickness. The simplest way to understand this is to experiment. Set the Outside Line, Middle Line, and Inside Line settings to, say, 5 points each using the scroll bars. Or make one of them 5 points and the others, say, 2 and 3. Then double-click on the Color/Fill box next to each line and choose a different fill color for each. Next to the words "Sample Line," you'll see the three-part line you've created. By typing in a description for this new line and selecting Save Line, you'll always have that special line style instantly available. If you check the Show In Menu box *before* selecting Save Line, you can even make your three-part line style appear on the menu you see when you select Lines.

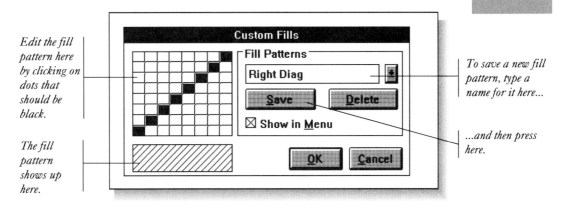

Edit the fill pattern here by clicking on dots that should be black.

The fill pattern shows up here.

To save a new fill pattern, type a name for it here...

...and then press here.

The Custom Fills Dialog Box

Rotate

Rotate, on the Effects menu, turns objects on the page. You can rotate simple shapes (boxes, lines, and polygons, for example), but not text or chart objects. And, once objects have been rotated, they can't be stretched, so always streeeeetch before you rotate.

The Rotate dialog box (it pops up when you select Rotate) lets you change the Degree of Rotation and specify the Vertical and Horizontal points around which the object should turn. The best way to understand these controls is to try different combinations and watch the effect on the sample box shown within the dialog box. To unrotate an object, set its degree of rotation to zero.

Shadow

Shadowing gives objects a three-dimensional effect. When you select

an object and then use Shadow on the Effects menu, the Shadow dialox box displays a sample rectangle along with scroll bars you can use to change the shadow's direction and its size. As an alternative, you can type in horizontal and vertical shadow numbers (positive numbers push the shadow to the right and down. Negative numbers push the shadow up and to the left. Using exact numbers rather than scroll bars is particularly helpful when you want the exact same shadow on several objects.

The rectangle in the lower right corner of the dialog box shows the current color of the shadow. Double-click on it to bring up the color palette if you want to change the shadow's color. ★

129

Using Color and Color Washes

▼

You can open the Color window at any time by pressing F6. If you want, push the Color window nearly off the screen to get it out of the way.

▼

To put a color wash in the background of a single page, double-click on the page and then use Color Wash on the Effects menu. Change the color scheme to put the same color wash in the background of every page.

Normally, the color scheme takes care of assigning colors to objects in Hollywood, but you can take on that job instead, simply by selecting the objects and then pressing F6 (the same as using Colors on the Effects menu). You'll see the color palette appear in its own window.

Immediately visible in the Color window are the sixteen basic colors of the VGA graphics system in an IBM PS/2 computer or the VGA or EGA card in some other brands of computer. If you stretch the color window so it becomes taller (or you if use the scroll bars to scroll through the color palette), you'll see a more detailed sequence of hues arranged in rainbow order (sorry, no pot of gold at the bottom).

To the left of the color palette are four buttons labeled Fill, Lines, Pattern, and Text. Click on one of these buttons to tell Hollywood which aspect of an object you want to colorize. Obviously, if you have a text object selected, you should select the Text button. A box, on the other hand, can have a pattern inside it (yellow dots, for example) that is different from the fill color (perhaps a dark red). To achieve this particular combination of colors, you'd select the box, choose dark red from the color palette, click on the button labeled Fill, and then select Apply on the Color Palette dialog box. Before selecting OK, you'd also select yellow from the color palette, click on the

Pattern button, and again select Apply.

Having the Apply button lets you apply different colors to different aspects of an object and then select OK only when you're finished.

Color Washes

A color wash is one of the snazziest effects Hollywood offers. It fills an object with gradations of color that start at one hue, gradually change to another, and then gradually change to still another, if you wish. A color wash can run horizontally across an object, vertically up or down an object, or radially, from the center of an object out to its edges. You also can apply a color wash to the background of every page in a presentation.

The Color Wash command on the Effects menu serves a dual purpose. With it, you can color an object with one of the color washes that are already set up, or you can create new color washes. To apply an existing color wash to an object, select the object, press the right mouse button to summon the Effects menu, and then select Color Wash. From the Color Wash dialog box that appears, select one of the color washes listed under Wash Name.

To define a new color wash, use the controls on the right side of the Color Wash dialog box. Click on the filled boxes next to Begin with, Go to, and End; that summons the color palette so you can select a color for each part of the wash. You don't need to use the

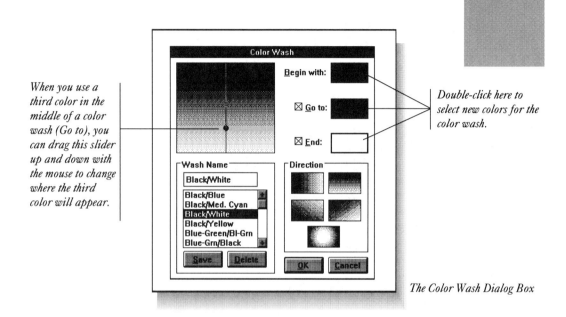

When you use a third color in the middle of a color wash (Go to), you can drag this slider up and down with the mouse to change where the third color will appear.

Double-click here to select new colors for the color wash.

The Color Wash Dialog Box

transitional Go-to color (you can leave the check box next to it unchecked), but if you do, you'll see a vertical line up the middle of the sample color wash with a dot along its length. Click on the dot and drag it up or down the line to change where along the color wash the transitional color comes in.

Finally, click on a direction for the color wash from the choices shown in the dialog box.

When you've finished defining a new color wash, replace the current wash name with a new one and then select Save in the dialog box. ★

Editing Colors in the Color Palette

You can change any color in the color palette to a slightly different shade by simply double-clicking on the color in the palette. Up pops the Edit Color dialog box, containing scroll bars you can manipulate to change the levels of red, green, and blue in the color. On the right, you'll see two filled boxes. The starting color appears in the top box and the changed color appears in the bottom one. When you're finished, select OK and your change is now permanent.

If you'd like, you can modify the cyan, yellow, and magenta values (CYM) of each color instead, or fiddle with their hue, saturation, and value levels (HSV). These are two alternate ways to specify color. Some people find the HSV control easiest to understand. It lets you first set the basic color of the spectrum (hue), and then determine its intensity (saturation) and then overall brightness (value).

Using Pictures in Hollywood

Images you've created can be saved in the Graphic Library. You'll probably want to re-create your company logo and save it in the Library, for example.

You can also import clip art images from commercial clip art libraries and then save your favorite images in the Graphic Library.

If you've got the artistic talent and training, you can draw your own pictures to accompany a presentation. But if you're like most of us, you'll be relieved to learn about Hollywood's Graphic Library. It's open to everybody.

The Graphic Library holds dozens of professionally drawn images covering a variety of subjects. You can use any of these images at any size and at any position on any page in your presentation. How's that for flexibility? You can even put them on the Master Page so that they show up on every page. And, if you've created a graphic image of your own that you may want to reuse in other presentations (your company logo, for example), you can copy it into the Graphic Library so that it's always available for use.

Borrowing from the Graphic Library

To select a picture from the library, use Graphic Library on the Special menu. The first six images in the library will show up in the Graphic Library window. Scroll through the rest of the images until you find just the right one. Then, click on it and select OK. The image appears in its own box on the current presentation page. Drag the box to a new location, or drag its handles to change the size of its box.

As you're scanning through the Graphic Library, you may want to examine an image a little more closely. If so, click on the image and then select Enlarge. When you're finished, press the spacebar to put it "back on the shelf." To delete an image from the library, select it and then select Delete.

Storing Pictures in the Library

To copy into the library an image you've created yourself, select it (this is easiest if you've used the Group command to join its component objects into one single object), and then select Copy from the Edit menu. Hollywood copies the image onto the Windows clipboard. Next, open the Graphic Library, click on the blank square at the end of the library, and select Paste from the Edit menu.

Don't try to copy a chart or a text object to the Graphic Library. It won't work. The only images the library can hold are ones made from shapes created with the Draw tool or clip art images you've imported into Hollywood from a clip art library.

Importing Graphics from Outside Hollywood

If the image you want to include in a presentation is in a file that is outside of Hollywood (part of a clip art library, perhaps, or the output from another graphics program), you can use Hollywood's Import Picture command to bring the image in and place it onto the current presentation page.

When you select Import Picture

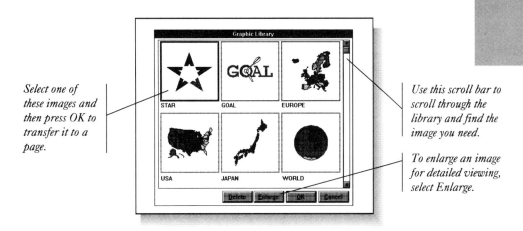

Select one of these images and then press OK to transfer it to a page.

Use this scroll bar to scroll through the library and find the image you need.

To enlarge an image for detailed viewing, select Enlarge.

The Graphic Library Window

from the File menu, you'll see a list of all the graphics files in the current directory. After you double-click on any of these filenames, you can place the picture on the page in one of two ways. One is to draw a box into which the image will go (this defines the positioning). The image appears. The second way is just to click on the page at the upper left corner of the spot where the image should go (this defines the placement of the image but uses the image's original size).

. After you've imported an image, you can double-click on it to transform it from a single object into individual graphic objects that you can modify with any of the drawing tools you've learned about in this chapter.

The images placed by the Hollywood installation process in the CLIPART, MAPS, and FLAGS subdirectories under the main Hollywood directory (HWOOD) are Computer Graphics Metafiles (CGM files). A CGM file is composed of a grouping of graphic objects. You'll probably be satisfied with the grouping just as is, but you can, if you wish, break apart the group so that you can modify the color, size, or shape of its component pieces.

After you've imported a CGM image onto a page, you can double-click on it to have Hollywood transform it from a collection of graphic shapes in CGM format to a collection of individual Hollywood graphic shapes. Hollywood will put a confirmation message on the screen. Click on OK to begin the process. Then, when it's done, you can individually select each of the image's component shapes , making all the changes you want. As always, you can use Hollywood's Group command to regroup the shapes when you're done making individual modifications. ★

Placing Graphics on the Master Page

The Master Page never makes an appearance in your presentation — at least not as a separate page. Instead, anything that's on it shows up on every page. For example, the Master Page gives you an easy way to place a line just below the title of every page. Place the line in the proper position on the Master Page and it shows up in the same position throughout the presentation.

To get to the Master Page, either use Master Page on the View menu, or else click on the page number at the bottom of the main presentation window and then, when the list of available pages appears, click on Master. Pressing Ctrl-G lets you jump quickly to a specific page of the presentation, but not to the Master Page.

Now you're free to draw on the Master Page, knowing you won't have to face the task of copying your drawing onto every page later. Of course, if you draw freehand on the Master Page, you'll be guessing how your artwork will align with other objects when it shows up on the regular presentation pages. You might, for example, want to place a a small design centered above each page title; working right on the Master Page, you won't know exactly where to position the boxes.

Rather than draw right on the Master Page in such a case, you might first want to add your graphic objects to a typical presentation page instead, so that you can properly align them with other objects on the page. Then you can use Cut on the Edit menu to remove them from the page and place them on the Windows Clipboard. Next, you'd select Master Page from the View menu and then select Paste to copy the graphic objects from the Clipboard to the same position on the Master Page. In essence, you've moved them from a typical page, where you were able to size and position them properly, to the Master Page, where you've now placed them so that they show up on every page.

The quickest way to leave the Master Page and return to a normal presentation page is to press Ctrl-G and then type in a presentation page number.

Hiding the Master Page

To avoid seeing the Master Page objects on a particular page, especially while you're still putting together that page, you can use Hide Master Page on the View menu while you're viewing that page. Now, as long as Hide Master Page is active, you won't see the Master Page graphics on that page. Back on the View menu, you can select Show Master Page to see

Go To...
✓ Master
1
2
3
4
5
6
7
8
9
PAGE # ← Master →

When you use a template to format a presentation, the template copies the contents of its Master Page onto your Master Page.

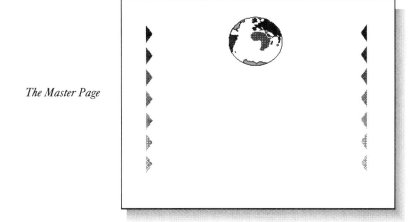

The Master Page

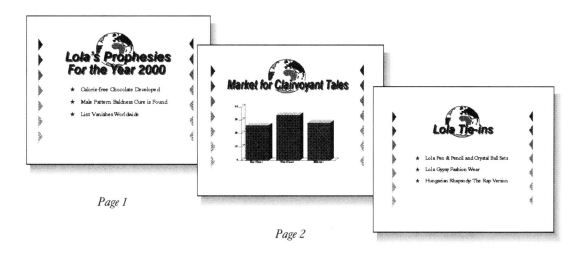

Page 1

Page 2

Page 3

the Master Page items once again. Hiding the Master Page items can be helpful because it takes Hollywood extra time to draw them onto your page. Each time you make a change to your page, Hollywood needs to redraw the Master Page items, too.

By temporarily hiding the Master Page objects, you can save that time. ★

Using the Object Specs Control

▼

The Object Specs control not only provides information about particular objects, but it lets you change their status, too.

▼

If you've customized the appearance of an object, make sure Use Color Scheme is not checked. If it is, the color scheme will reformat the object according to its instructions.

You've learned that nearly every object you place on a Hollywood page has a set of options. In addition, every object also has a set of object specs. They specify the object's exact size and location on the page and determine whether that object is controlled by the color scheme.

When you click on an object and then use Object Specs on the View menu, you'll see a dialog box that shows two sets of controls — one that reflects the object's current position in the presentation and one that reflects its size.

An Object's Position

The Position on Page controls tell you the precise location of the object by specifying the exact spot where its upper left handle appears when that object is selected. X Across measures how far the handle is from the left side of the page, and Y Down measures how far it is from the top of the page. Layer # specifies the layer on which the object is placed. You can change any of these values to accurately reposition the object rather than dragging it with the mouse.

An Object's Size

The Object Size controls show the width and height of the object in the current measurement units. Once again, change these numbers to directly affect the object.

Two check boxes at the bottom of the dialog box let you restrict the size and positioning of the object (Lock Object Specs) and specify whether the appearance of the object should be governed by the current color scheme (Use Color Scheme).

With the object specs locked, it's impossible for any of Hollywood's tools to change the size or position of that object.

Overriding the Color Scheme

When the Use Color Scheme box is checked, the object's design is governed by the color scheme. Any time you make a local change to the design of an object, though, Hollywood automatically unchecks the Use Color Scheme box for you. Local changes are those you make by selecting the object and then using the commands on the Type or Effects menus. When you make a local change to an object, Hollywood recognizes that you want to override the global color scheme. While Use Color Scheme remains unchecked, your change takes precedence over the color scheme's design rules. Should you want to let the color scheme take control of the object once again, select the object and then select Use Color Scheme so the Use Color Scheme box is checked once again. ★

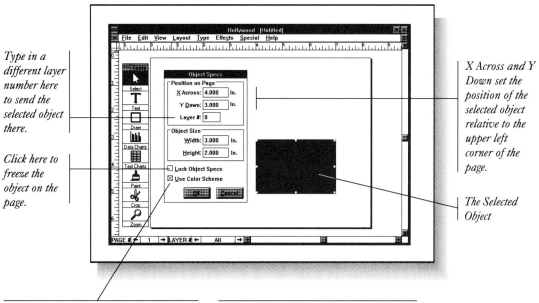

Type in a different layer number here to send the selected object there.

Click here to freeze the object on the page.

X Across and Y Down set the position of the selected object relative to the upper left corner of the page.

The Selected Object

Make sure this box is unchecked to prevent the color scheme from undoing a change you've made. Hollywood should take care of this automatically, but take a look here to be sure.

To abandon the changes you've made and let the color scheme regain control of the object, make sure the box next to Use Color Scheme is checked.

Where To from Here?

✓ Outlining the Presentation
✓ Adding Bullet and Data
     Charts
✓ Adding Other Chart Types
✓ Adding the Trimmings: Extra
     Text and Graphics
Next: Formatting the Presentation
     Showing Off Your Work

Your presentation now has all the text charts, data charts, text, and graphics it needs. Time to learn how you can modify the color scheme or apply a template to change the overall appearance of the presentation. That's up next.

BEHIND THE SCENES

Using Color Schemes,
Templates, and Preferences

In This Chapter

$\blacklozenge$

What Are Color Schemes, Templates, and Preferences?

Y ou could, if you want, quickly throw together a bunch of charts and graphs and be done with it — but what a waste of Hollywood's powers that would be! You only need to consider Just look at the Outliner to recognize how much more you can do with Hollywood.

The Outliner, as you know, lets you marshal the flow of a presentation's ideas, guiding the way they evolve from one page to the next. That helps you unify the *content*. But several other key Hollywood components can help you unify the *design*, too, so your pages have a consistent appearance.

This chapter will help you master these design-related parts of Hollywood—the color scheme, the template, and preferences—so you'll have a presentation that's not only clear and comprehensible, but uniform and professional-looking, too.

The Color Scheme

The most important of Hollywood's design components, the color scheme, stores a different collection of design rules for each *category* of object in a presentation. A typical design rule might say, "For all the data chart titles in this presentation, set the font to 14-point Swiss bold." The category in this case is "data chart titles." (Other elements the color scheme might control are colors and line styles; it all depends on which

elements are used in that category.)

Another category the program can apply a set of rules to is the set of shapes you create with Hollywood's Draw tools. Each element of each chart type is yet another category: the color scheme holds one set of design rules for bullet chart titles, for example, and a different set for table chart titles, though the designs are probably similar.

Because a color scheme applies the same design rules to every object of each type throughout the entire presentation, the sequence of pages takes on a uniform look. What's more, you can quickly impart an entirely new design to an existing presentation simply by picking a different color scheme, thereby modifying all objects in each category. That can be important, for example, when you need to print an all-color presentation on a black-and-white laser printer. By switching to the color scheme designed for a laser printer, you can have Hollywood replace colors with shades of gray.

The Template

Applying a different color scheme is enough to radically change the look of a presentation. But applying a template goes even further.

A template is a presentation that you've saved to use as a model for future presentations. When you call up a template, either before you begin a presentation or after, it does these things:

☆ It applies the *color scheme* of the original presentation to the new presentation.

☆ It moves the charts and graphic objects of your new presentation to the same *positions* they occupied in the original presentation.

☆ It sets the *options* of your new objects to match the options of similar objects in the original presentation.

☆ It copies the contents of the original presentation's *Master Page* to the new presentation's Master Page.

So, a template not only affects the design of objects (by applying a color scheme and changing the objects' options), but it sets the design of entire pages, too (through the color scheme and the Master Page). That leaves you with little to do except decide on the types of charts you need, create them, and then modestly deflect the praise of your colleagues.

Preferences

A preference file is a starting configuration for Hollywood. It specifies several settings for the *next* presentation you start, and it sets up most of Hollywood's operating parameters. Some of the settings that are stored in the preference file have to do with the *design* of the next presentation:

☆ the size and orientation of the main page, and

☆ the color scheme that will be in effect.

And some have to do with how Hollywood will *work*:

☆ the default settings for each of Hollywood's tools;

☆ the output device the presentation should be tailored for (a black-and-white laser printer, a color printer, or a film recorder, for example);

☆ the position of all the windows within the main Hollywood window (the Toolbox window, main presentation window, and the color palette window); and

☆ the settings for the rulers and grid.

Once again, changes you make to a preference file will affect the *next* presentation you create, not the current one. You can override any of these individual settings after you start the presentation—changing the color scheme or the page size, for example—but once you've started a presentation, you can't try a different preference on it.

Whenever you start Hollywood, it loads the last preference you used, even if that was some time ago. You can choose a different preference for today's work as long as you do it before you start a new presentation.

The next two pages go into some typical scenarios for using a preference file, template, and color scheme together. ★

Using Preferences, Templates, and Color Schemes Together

The most automatic way to use preferences, templates, and color schemes is to select a preference file and template file before you start creating text and data charts. Then, as you add each chart, Hollywood formats and positions it, leaving you with little to do.

Here are three typical ways you might employ a preference file, a template, and a color scheme as you create a new presentation. The approach you take depends on the material you're dealing with or your personal preference. The first one is called...

Scenario One: Preference First, Content Next, and a Little More Design

First, you choose a preference file from among those available. (Hollywood comes with a starter set of preference files, but you can add to it.) That sets up the basic presentation page, establishes the output device your presentation should be tailored for, and applies a color scheme that matches the output device. Two aspects of your design are now taken care of: the format of the basic page and the color scheme.

Next, you go into the Outliner, create a series of presentation pages, and then add data charts, table charts, and tree charts to the pages wherever you'd like. You might also add graphic objects directly to the pages, or perhaps place them on the Master Page so that they repeat throughout the presentation. In this scenario, you still need to decide a number of things for yourself: exactly where on each page each chart should go, for instance, and how to ornament the

presentation with graphic design elements (perhaps a beveled rectangle at the top of each page, placed under each page title, or a design across the top and bottom of each page).

Scenario Two: Preference File and Template First, Content Second

In another scenario, you let the template decide where the charts should go. As before, first you choose a preference file, but then you select a template for the presentation, too. The template automatically sets up the Master Page and the color scheme; then, as you add charts to the pages, the template intervenes, deciding where they should go and how they should look. The template even sets their options. Here, the preference file and the template take care of nearly everything about the design, leaving you to concentrate exclusively on the content. This scenario is the most desirable as it's the most automatic.

Scenario Three: Content First, Design Second

In yet another scenario, you don't even bother with the Preferences command. You always use the same preference file because it's set up for your one and only output device, and it specifies a color scheme and page format that work well with that output device.

SCENARIO 1

You do:

1. *Select a preference file.*
2. *Enter outline into Outliner, use Draw Chart, and add other charts.*

Hollywood does:

1. *Preference file applies a color scheme.*

You must still:

1. *Position text and data charts on the page.*
2. *Place ornamentation on the Master Page.*
3. *Make fine-tuning adjustments.*

SCENARIO 2

You do:

1. *Select a preference file.*
2. *Get a template for the presentation.*
3. *Enter outline into Outliner, use Draw Chart, and add other charts.*

Hollywood does:

1. *Preference file applies a color scheme.*
2. *Places its Master Page graphics on your Master Page.*
3. *Positions each chart as you add it.*

You must still:

1. *Make fine-tuning adjustments.*

SCENARIO 3

You do:

1. *Always use the same preference file.*
2. *Enter outline into Outliner, use Draw Chart, and add other charts.*
3. *Try different templates to apply different presentation designs.*

Hollywood does:

1. *Preference file applies a color scheme.*
2. *Template files you try rearrange the presentation and place different graphics on the Master Page.*

You must still:

1. *Make fine-tuning adjustments.*

Instead, you concentrate on the content of the presentation by using the Outliner, the Data Chart tools, and the Text Chart tools, and then you try applying a few different templates you've used in the past, to see which one you prefer. You can even use different templates for different versions of the same presentation: one that applies a bold, jazzy design for your associates, and another that applies a more serious-minded design for the board of directors.

Each of these scenarios is equally valid. You can take as much help from preferences and templates as you want, or just tell them to stay out of the way while you cook up a new design of your own. In the remainder of this chapter, we'll focus in detail on these three tools: preferences, templates, and color schemes. ★

Choosing and Setting Up Preferences

The best time to deal with preference files is when you first sit down for a Hollywood session — especially if someone else has been using your Hollywood while you were away. You want to be sure the correct preference file is loaded *before* you start a new presentation. With that done, you probably won't need to think about preferences for a while; the current preference file stays active until you choose a different one, even if that's many sessions with Hollywood later.

By selecting Preferences on the File menu, you get to an expandable dialog box that lists preference files for a handful of standard presentation formats.

After you choose a preference, you may want to make a change or two to its settings. Select More to expand the Preferences dialog box, and you'll see the full array of preference settings.

Preference Settings

The Preference Files setting, at the top left corner of the dialog box, is joined by a number of other settings as soon as you select More. Page Format lets you choose from among three built-in page heights and widths: Screen (designed for showing your presentation right on the computer screen), Overhead (for creating transparencies, or "foils"), and 35mm Slide. A fourth choice, Custom, lets you enter a page format of your own. You'll notice that if you try to change the Height or Width of

any format, the Page Format instantly switches to Custom. You'll also see that you can't change the orientation of the Screen or 35mm Slide page formats. They're both landscape (horizontal) rather than portrait (vertical). But you *can* choose either portrait or landscape for overheads.

On Startup Load determines what Hollywood does when you first start the program: it either loads the last presentation you saved or starts with a new presentation (using the current preference file, of course).

The Color Scheme setting lets you assign a color scheme to the preference file. Pages Per Handout is useful when you want your audience to go home with miniature copies of your presentation. This setting lets you determine how many miniature presentation pages — from one to six — Hollywood will print on each handout page.

Measurement gives you a choice of four possible units of measure Hollywood can use (inches, picas, points, and centimeters), both in all of its dialog boxes and in the rulers on the screen. Whichever unit you choose will be applied across the board: to dialog boxes and rulers.

Output Device lets you specify which of the output devices currently installed in Windows you plan to use to produce your presentation. Remember, though: whichever device you choose here should also be chosen under Printer Setup on the File menu. Hollywood uses these two settings to determine, among

Remember, changing the preference file will affect the next presentation you start. The current presentation was set up by the old preference file.

Create preference files for all of your output devices to make Hollywood foolproof.

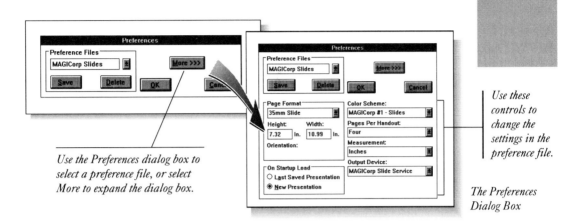

Use the Preferences dialog box to select a preference file, or select More to expand the dialog box.

Use these controls to change the settings in the preference file.

The Preferences Dialog Box

other things, which fonts are available in your printer. Then it makes only those fonts available on the font list.

Creating a Preference File

You'll want to create a preference file of your own once you've become familiar with Hollywood. One day, before you begin working in Hollywood, take a minute or two and create a preference file that has the program set just the way you like it. Now, unless you switch to a different preference file, you'll find everything set when you begin each new presentation.

To create a preference file of your own, first set up some of Hollywood's basic operating conditions: move the Toolbox to a comfortable position on the screen, hide or show the ruler,

position the main presentation and color windows where you want them, and make any changes you'd like to the defaults of each tool. For example, if you always want column charts to have a half-inch 3D effect, press Ctrl when you select the Column Chart tool; that brings up the Column Chart options dialog box, showing the default options settings for column charts so that you can make that change.

Then, you should choose Preferences on the File menu and make any changes you need to the preferences settings. Finally, type a new name for the preference file in the text box under Preference Files, and then select Save. Remember, you won't see most of these changes take effect until you start a brand-new presentation. ★

Overriding a Preference

At any time while you're using Hollywood, you can override some of the preference file's settings by using Page Setup on the File menu. The settings for Page Format, Pages

Per Handout, and Output Device appear in the Page Setup dialog box. Unlike changing the preferences settings, changing any of these will have an immediate impact on the current presentation.

Applying a Template

M aybe one of your presentations was particularly successful and you'd like to borrow its design for a new one. Or perhaps it's time to give one of your old presentations a complete design overhaul based on a proven pattern. Either goal can be accomplished by applying a template: an old presentation you've stored away just so you can use it as a model.

Old Wardrobe, New Plot

How you apply a template depends on whether you've already created the pages or are just about to. If making the pages still lies ahead, applying a template is easy. You simply select Get Template on the Special menu and choose the template you want. As you create the presentation, the template works behind the scenes, instituting an overall design and placing the charts you add at just the right position on each page.

If, however, your aim is to apply a template to a presentation you've already got, you may need to help Hollywood along as it works.

Re-dressing a Classic

Here's how a template works when you ask it to process pages you've already got: As you turn to each page of the presentation, the template tries to find a match among its own pages. If a page has two items—a page title and a table chart, for example—the template searches through its pages for one with the same combination. If

it finds such a page, it applies the arrangement of that page to yours. If it finds more than one such page, it pops open a dialog box that lets you scroll through and choose from among the pages it found. If it finds no matching page at all, it does not change the position of the objects on your page. That's up to you.

The obvious hitch to this scheme is that Hollywood can't always automatically apply a template to every page of an existing presentation. Instead, you must view each of the pages one by one so that the template can size it up. And you can't stop until you've seen every page of the presentation. But for that trouble, you get a presentation with a design you have faith in — and one that's completely formatted in far less time than if you'd done it manually.

Getting Specific

Several steps are required to apply a template to an existing presentation — but Hollywood really does most of the work.

First, before selecting a template, turn to the first page of the presentation (click on the current page number at the bottom of the presentation window and then select "1" from the list of pages). Then, use Get Template on the Special menu to select a template file. Be sure to look in the special Templates subdirectory that the Hollywood installation program sets up under the main Hollywood directory (HWOOD). If you're unsure which template to

The best time to apply a template is when you start a presentation. Then, the template formats each chart as you create it.

You can also apply templates to existing presentations to give them a complete design overhaul.

Original Presentation

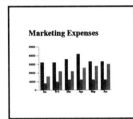

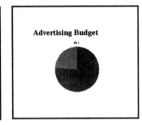

Attaching this template to the presentation above produces...

Master Page

Bullet Chart Page

Column Chart Page

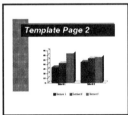

Pie Chart Page

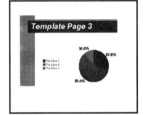

Presentation with Template Attached

...these charts automatically.

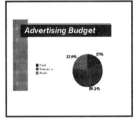

choose, select one of the templates you think you might want and then select Show Sample so you can preview its design. You can use the scroll bar on the right to scroll through the template's pages.

After you've selected a template, Hollywood evaluates the first page of your presentation. If it finds a simple match among the template's pages, the template does its stuff. If there are two or more matches, the template pops open a dialog box showing the first of the alternative pages. Scroll through the pages until you find the design you want, and then select OK. Now, repeat the process for each of the pages in your presentation. It won't take as long as it sounds. An average-length presentation can be completely formatted in a minute or two.

To remove the effects of a template, you can always select Get Template again (on the Special menu) and then check the box marked "Don't use template." ★

Creating a Template File

B y now you have a sense of the power of Hollywood templates. A template can take over virtually every decision that needs to be made about a presentation's design, leaving you free to concentrate on its content.

Hollywood comes with a starter set of templates, but you can always create custom templates with designs appropriate for your work.

Creating a basic template is easy: just design a presentation you like and then save it as a template. In the future, when you apply that template to another presentation, the new presentation will adopt the design of your first one — the one you liked so much.

Here are the steps: First, create a presentation, complete with a color scheme, Master Page design, and charts placed on pages. Next, save the presentation as you normally would (using Save on the File menu, typing in a name for the presentation, and then making sure Save As Presentation is selected on the Save dialog box). Now, go back to the Save command, but this time make sure to select Save As Template on the Save dialog box. You can even use the same name for the template as you've used for the presentation. Hollywood assigns an .HWT file extension ("T" for "template") to the saved file rather than the usual .HWD file extension. ("D" doesn't stand for anything. "HWD" is short for "Hollywood.")

Now, if what you want is a template that can automatically handle just about any presentation you might throw at it — that takes a little more work. You'll have to follow a few guidelines before saving your presentation as a template.

First, make sure you haven't included any duplicate designs in the presentation (for example, two pages that have both a page title and a tree chart). The best way to ensure this is to check it out in Presentation View, which shows you a miniature of each page and lets you delete pages quickly. You'll learn about Presentation View in the next chapter. Then, choose Save As Template when you save the file. The template may not have all the pages of the original presentation, but really, you don't need them: if you think of the template as a collection of page designs, you'll understand that you need only as many pages as you have separate designs.

Creating a Comprehensive Template

You may also want to adapt a presentation so that it's super-powered: capable of handling virtually any combination of objects you might encounter in a future presentation. For this, you'll want to create a master presentation with enough pages in it so that each possible combination of objects has a representative page. Again, the first

A comprehensive template has enough pages to match any combination of charts you place on a page.

Templates are large files, so create just the ones you'll need.

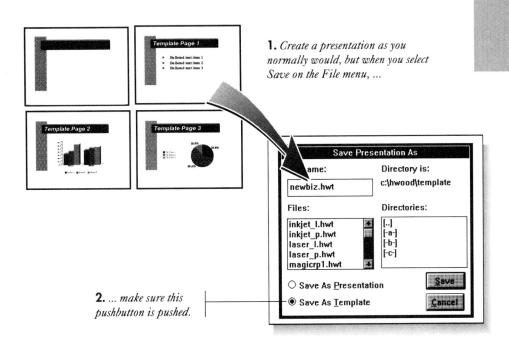

1. *Create a presentation as you normally would, but when you select Save on the File menu, ...*

2. *... make sure this pushbutton is pushed.*

steps are best done in Presentation View. There, you can copy pages so that you have several of each type. Then you can go to the page copies and vary their design until you've covered all possible permutations. When you're done, you should have a presentation that takes into account just about any combination of charts you're likely to have on a page.

Beware, though, that comprehensive templates, because they have so many pages, will be unusually large files. Make sure you have plenty of space on your hard disk before trying to create and store too many comprehensive templates. ★

Buying New Templates

Normally, you make templates by saving your own custom presentation designs. But you may want to acquire custom templates that have been professionally designed by a graphic artist. At the back of this book you'll find information about just such a thing: sets of professionally designed templates for various styles of presentation that you can purchase using the order form. These are comprehensive templates that will format just about any presentation from top to bottom. They'll be a worthwhile addition to your Hollywood package.

Selecting a Color Scheme

P
references set Hollywood up. Templates design the overall presentation. And color schemes design your charts.

Color Schemes, on the Effects menu, gives you an entire arsenal of chart designs from which to choose. When the Color Schemes dialog box pops open, you see two things: a control for selecting a color scheme, and a miniature of the presentation's background page, with both a text object and a graphic object placed on top. This first dialog box may let you do all you'll want to do with color schemes: select one of the existing color schemes and check out the miniature to see some of its effects.

But by selecting More, you can instantly expand the dialog box to show a complete second tier of settings—additional controls that let you modify existing color schemes and create new ones.

On this page and the next you'll find information about how to select a color scheme and apply it to a presentation. The remaining pages of this chapter tell you how to use the rest of the controls to customize color schemes for your particular needs.

Radical Changes

Changing a presentation's color scheme can radically change the appearance of every object in the presentation. It all depends on how the color scheme has been set up. Picture a color scheme as working like this: It starts at the beginning of the

presentation, determining the chart type of the first chart it comes across. Next, the color scheme looks up its design rules for that chart type and applies the assigned colors, color washes, line styles, and fill patterns. Then it continues with the next chart. Somewhere along the way, it also looks up its design rules for the background page (called the main page by the color scheme) and for the objects on the background page, and it changes their appearance, too.

The design rules stored in the color scheme are different things altogether from the options of charts and of objects you've drawn. Options determine an object's configuration (whether the bars of a column chart are stacked on top of one another, for example, or whether arrowheads should appear at the ends of a line). The color scheme makes decisions about how that configuration will look, such as which colors will appear in the bars of a column chart.

Now, understand that the design choices made by a color scheme are not etched in granite. Most can be overridden, object by object. What color schemes give you, then, is the consistency of a uniform design combined with the flexibility to contradict the color scheme's design when need be.

What's Best for the Printer

Color schemes provide yet another benefit of importance: each can optimize a presentation for a different

---

▼

You can use the miniature in the Color Schemes dialog box to see the effects of the color scheme.

▼

Color schemes format categories of objects. You can still select a single object and then format it with Hollywood's menu commands.

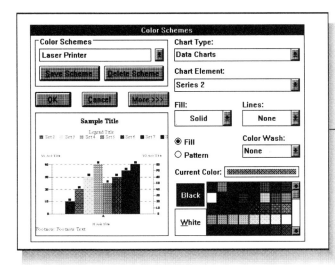

This color scheme (for black-and-white printers) is setting all the series in the data charts to different shades of gray.

Series 1 in each data chart is a very dark gray. Series 2 is a lighter shade of gray. Series 3 is lighter still.

The color scheme sees to it that every data chart you create gets the same selection of colors.

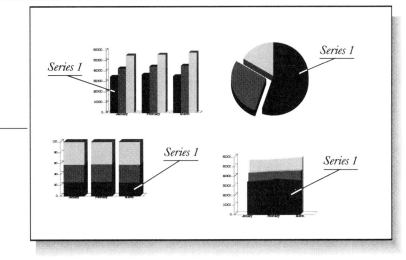

output device you have on hand. One color scheme can have a broad range of vibrant colors for your color inkjet printer, for example. Another can translate colors into shades of gray for a dot matrix or laser printer. By simply changing the color scheme attached to a presentation, you can instantly prepare the presentation for output on a different device. ★

Setting Up a Color Scheme

A s with templates and preferences, Hollywood comes with a starter selection of color schemes you can use. But you'll soon want to customize these schemes or design your own. Customizing a color scheme takes only a few logical steps.

A color scheme can be customized at any time during a Hollywood work session. Color Schemes on the Effects menu shows you a small dialog box with a control for choosing one of the color schemes that are already set up. By selecting More, you can expand the dialog box to see the controls that let you modify a color scheme.

Taking Each Chart Type in Turn

At the right side of this newly expanded Color Scheme dialog box is the Chart Type setting, with a list you can open to reveal these choices: Bullet Chart, Data Charts, Main Page, Table Chart, and Tree Chart. Obviously, "Main Page," in the middle of the list, is not really a chart type, but it *is* an aspect of a presentation that can be formatted with a color scheme. As you select each chart type, the sample page on the left displays a miniature of it. That miniature will show you each change you make to the design of the chart.

What Changes, What Won't

After you select a chart type, use the Chart Element control to see all the customizable components of that chart type. For example, if you choose Bullet Chart, the Chart Element list displays Bullet Color, Sub-title Type Style and Color, and Title Type Style and Color: three things you can customize about bullet charts. To see which elements can be customized in each chart type, try selecting the different chart types and then looking at the Chart Element list.

Below the Chart Element list are the settings you can change to customize each chart element. Which settings you'll see depend on which chart element you're designing. If you're setting up the appearance of bullet chart titles, for example, you'll see Type Style and Current Color settings; but when you're setting up the bullets, only the Current Color setting is available for you to change.

When you're customizing an element that can have both a fill color and a pattern color, such as a graphic object on the main page, two pushbuttons become available. They're labeled, not surprisingly, Fill and Pattern. Select one of these pushbuttons before you select a color from the color palette.

Some of the design-setting controls let you pick from among preexisting text styles and color washes. If you have in mind a text style or color wash that's not already set up, you had better go set it up first, before trying to use it in a color scheme, because you can't create a new type style or

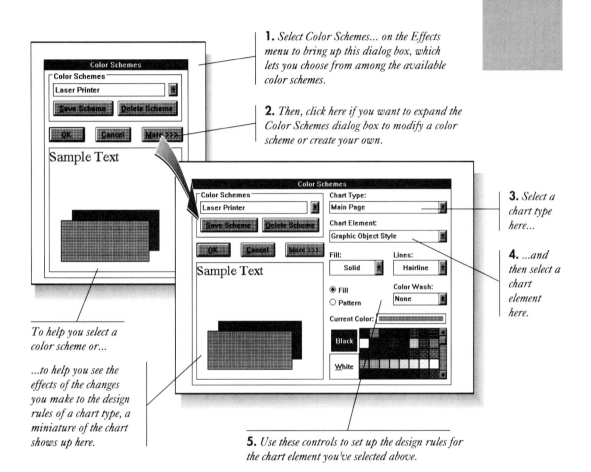

1. *Select Color Schemes... on the Effects menu to bring up this dialog box, which lets you choose from among the available color schemes.*

2. *Then, click here if you want to expand the Color Schemes dialog box to modify a color scheme or create your own.*

3. *Select a chart type here...*

4. *...and then select a chart element here.*

To help you select a color scheme or...

...to help you see the effects of the changes you make to the design rules of a chart type, a miniature of the chart shows up here.

5. *Use these controls to set up the design rules for the chart element you've selected above.*

color wash while you're working in the Color Schemes dialog box.

Any changes you make to the color scheme settings will affect the current presentation immediately, but you'll probably want to save your customized color scheme for use on future presentations. To save a color scheme you've modified, type a new name for it over the existing name and then select Save Scheme on the Color Schemes dialog box. To delete a color scheme you no longer want, select it and then select Delete Scheme.

The next three sets of pages will take you through the various chart types, explaining the color scheme settings you'll find for each. ★

Bullet Chart and Data Chart
Color Scheme Entries

O n these two pages, and on the next two, you'll find a picture of each chart type with all of its chart elements identified. Below each chart is a table that lists each chart element and the characteristics of that element that you can set in the color scheme. ★

Remember, change the color scheme to modify one chart and all the charts of the same type change.

To override the color scheme for a single chart, though, make sure Use Color Scheme under Object Specs is off.

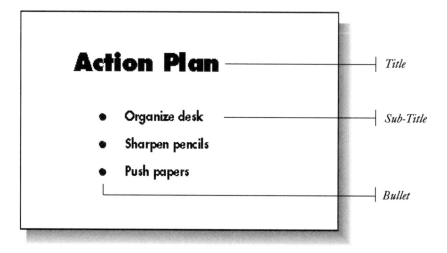

Bullet Chart

Bullet Chart	
Bullet Color	Fill, Color Wash, Fill Color, Pattern Color
Sub-Title Type Style & Color	Type Style, Current Color
Title Type Style & Color	Type Style, Current Color

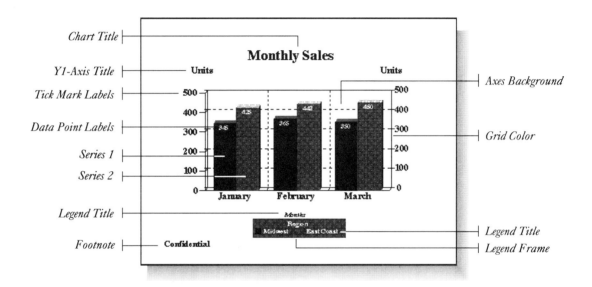

Data Chart

Data Charts			
Axes Background	Fill, Color Wash, Fill Color, Pattern Color	Series 3	Fill, Lines, Color Wash, Fill Color, Pattern Color
Chart Title	Type Style, Current Color	Series 4	Fill, Lines, Color Wash, Fill Color, Pattern Color
Data Point Labels	Type Style, Current Color	Series 5	Fill, Lines, Color Wash, Fill Color, Pattern Color
Footnotes	Type Style, Current Color	Series 6	Fill, Lines, Color Wash, Fill Color, Pattern Color
Grid Color	Current Color	Series 7	Fill, Lines, Color Wash, Fill Color, Pattern Color
Legend Frame	Fill, Lines, Color Wash, Fill Color, Pattern Color	Series 8	Fill, Lines, Color Wash, Fill Color, Pattern Color
Legend Title	Type Style, Current Color	Tick Mark Labels	Type Style, Current Color
Series 1	Fill, Lines, Color Wash, Fill Color, Pattern Color	X-Axis Title	Type Style, Current Color
Series 2	Fill, Lines, Color Wash, Fill Color, Pattern Color	Y1-Axis Title	Type Style, Current Color
Series 3	Fill, Lines, Color Wash, Fill Color, Pattern Color	Y2-Axis Title	Type Style, Current Color

Main Page, Table Chart, and Tree Chart Color Scheme Entries

The main page isn't really a chart, of course, but color schemes classify it as one so they can control its appearance.

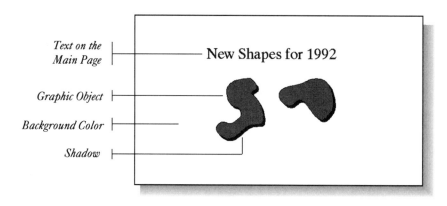

Text on the Main Page

Graphic Object

Background Color

Shadow

New Shapes for 1992

Main Page	
Graphic Object Style	Fill, Color Wash, Fill Color, Pattern Color
Page Background Color	Fill, Color Wash, Fill Color, Pattern Color
Shadow Fill and Color	Fill, Fill Color, Pattern Color
Text Type Style and Color	Type Style, Current Color

Table charts and tree charts are composed of many objects. You can directly format any cell in a table chart or any leaf in a tree chart.

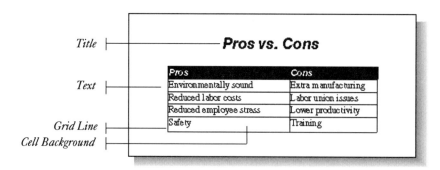

Title

Text

Grid Line

Cell Background

Pros vs. Cons

Pros	Cons
Environmentally sound	Extra manufacturing
Reduced labor costs	Labor union issues
Reduced employee stress	Lower productivity
Safety	Training

Table Chart	
Cell Background Color	Current Color
Grid Line Color	Current Color
Text Type Style & Color	Type Style, Current Color
Title Type Style & Color	Type Style, Current Color

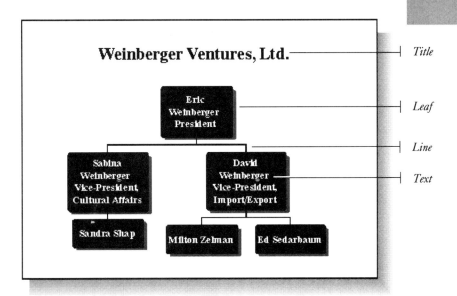

Title

Leaf

Line

Text

Tree Chart	
Leaf Style	Fill, Lines, Color Wash, Fill Color, Pattern Color
Line Style	Lines
Text Type Style & Color	Type Style, Current Color
Title Type Style & Color	Type Style, Current Color

Where To from Here?

✓ Outlining the Presentation
✓ Adding Bullet and Data
   Charts
✓ Adding Other Chart Types
✓ Adding the Trimmings: Extra
   Text and Graphics
✓ Formatting the Presentation
Next: Showing Off Your Work

   Now it's time for the rest of the world to see the spectacular presentation you've crafted. You'll learn all about creating screen shows and producing printed output and slides in the next two chapters.

Roll 'Em!

Producing Screen Shows

In This Chapter

◆

What Is a Hollywood Screen Show?

The form a presentation takes depends in large part on how you plan to show it. Will you print it on pages and copy them onto overhead transparencies? Will you send it to a slide maker or a service bureau to make slides? Or will you pass out printed copies and have your audience turn the pages as you speak?

Usually, it's a combination of the equipment you've got on hand (if any) and the audience you'll be speaking to that determines how to present a presentation. You'll certainly have a more professional appearance if you walk in with a crisp, colorful set of slides rather than with plain old black-and-white overheads. But to show slides you'll need a slide projector, not just a simple overhead projector. What's more, you'll need to prepare your slide presentation well in advance and spend the extra money having slides made, while overheads are inexpensive to produce and you can tinker with them right up until the last minute.

A Silver Screen Presentation

One alternative to both slides and overheads — and the subject of this chapter — is to show your Hollywood charts directly from the computer. A Hollywood screen show gives you fancy colors and up-to-the-last-minute changes, and best of all, it lets you blend from chart to chart with dazzling video transition effects such as dissolves, wipes, and pans.

If your audience is small, perhaps a few people in a meeting room, and you have a computer with a large color screen, then a screen show may be just the ticket. And even if your audience is large, you can use a video projector to project a computer's images onto a big screen. Many computer projectors can even hook into the back of a portable computer, which means you can bring a presentation with you that is all set and ready for the big silver screen.

Point by Point

To deliver a series of points about a topic, you may well have packaged them neatly in a bullet chart. With the traditional methods of showing bullet charts (slides, handouts, or overhead transparencies), you'd either show the completed bullet chart all at once, or you might start with a chart that shows only one point, then advance to the next page or slide for each new point. Each new page adds yet another point to the bottom of the list of points already covered.

But for real Hollywood drama, why not use a screen show and let Hollywood add each point right on the screen? Each new point could fade into view or wipe onto the screen brightly. At the same time, the points you've already completed could fade to a darker, more muted color.

Take It from Bar Three

If you're presenting graphic data charts, Hollywood can progressively build them too, adding each new set

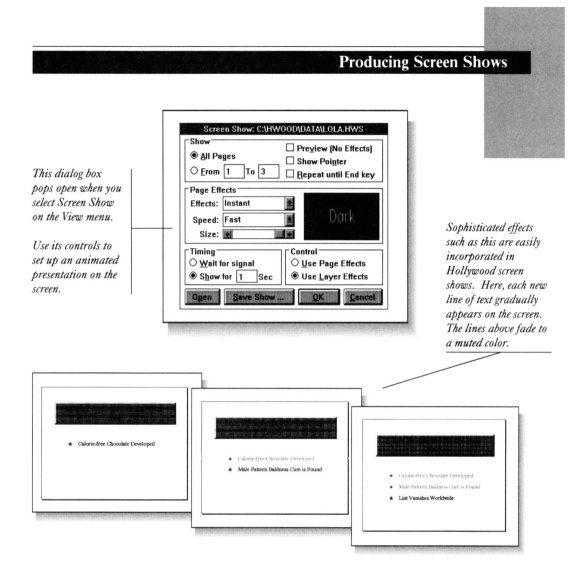

This dialog box pops open when you select Screen Show on the View menu.

Use its controls to set up an animated presentation on the screen.

Sophisticated effects such as this are easily incorporated in Hollywood screen shows. Here, each new line of text gradually appears on the screen. The lines above fade to a muted color.

A Portion of a Screen Show Already in Progress

of bars or each new pie slice to the ones already showing on the screen. Imagine, for example, that you must explain the breakdown of a set of clients. Rather than show a completed pie chart and methodically point by hand to each slice, why not reveal each slice one at a time as you describe it? A little drama can go a long way.

Hollywood makes creating such progressive builds easy. Just turn on the Progressive Build option in the chart's dialog box and Hollywood does all the work.

You'll learn about progressive builds, and everything else about screen shows, in the remainder of this chapter. ★

Creating a Simple Screen Show

O ne screen show you might want to create is a simple progression through the pages of your presentation, using a fancy transition from one page to the next.

When you're ready to turn a presentation into a screen show, first take a quick look at it in Presentation

A simple screen show that's easy to set up can simply progress from one page to the next using the same transition effect each time.

View	
Zoom In	F7
Actual Size	Ctrl+V
Zoom Out	F8
√ Size To Fit	Ctrl+W
Redraw	Ctrl+R
√ Page	
Notes Page	
Handout Page	
Master Page	
Data Table/Outline	Ctrl+D
Options...	
Object Specs...	
Presentation...	
Screen Show...	

View. Make sure that the pages are in the correct order and that you've included everything you need and nothing that's extraneous. Then, select Screen Show from the View menu while you're viewing any of the presentation pages.

You'll see the Screen Show dialog box with its four groups of controls: Show, Page Effects, Timing, and Control. They set the transition effects between images and set a few other characteristics of the screen show.

The Show Controls

The Show controls determine, among other things, which portion of a presentation you'll see when you start the show. Preview gives you a sequential look at your pages without transition effects. When you select Preview and then select OK, Hollywood shows you your presentation one page at time,

To create a more complex screen show, with bars that wipe up and pie slices that fade into view, you must use layers and layer effects, described later in this chapter.

without any special transition effects. This gives you a chance to see what the flow of pages feels like so you can think about what kinds of transition effects you want to use. After you've looked at the first page, you must press the right arrow key to move forward a page.

Selecting Show Pointer leaves the mouse cursor on the screen while a screen show is running so you can point with it to items in your charts. Selecting Repeat Until End Key means the show will be displayed over and over until you press the End key; perfect for a demonstration that should run continuously, perhaps in a store window or an exhibit.

The Page Effects Controls

The Page Effects controls determine the special transition effect that will be used to reveal every page. Open the list next to Effects and you'll see sixteen different choices. As you select each effect, the sample to the right uses that effect to switch back and forth between two images (labeled "Light" and "Dark"), demonstrating how the transition will look.

On the list next to Speed, you'll find three different transition speeds to control the pace of the effect (slow, medium, and fast).

The effect of the Size control depends on the transition effect you've chosen. If you've selected Blinds as the transition effect, for example, the Size control determines whether they appear as large Venetian blinds or small mini-blinds. Generally, a smaller size takes longer to happen on the screen. You'll need to experiment with both the Speed and Size controls to get a transition speed that looks right to you.

The Timing Controls

Hollywood can wait until you press a key or mouse button before changing to the next page (Wait for Signal), or in an unattended presentation, each page can be displayed for a set amount of time (Show for __ Sec). Use Wait for Signal if you'll be using the keyboard or a mouse during the show to control its pacing.

Page Effects or Layer Effects?

When you choose Use Page Effects in the Control group, the page effect you select will be used throughout the entire presentation. If you've built your pages out of layers and specified a transition effect for each layer, you can choose Use Layer Effects, instead. You'll be learning all about layers and layer effects on the next few pages.

Running the Show

You can now select OK to view your presentation as a screen show. Unless you've selected Preview, Hollywood

displays a message box labeled "Building Screen Show" as it creates your show with all its effects. When the show is ready, Hollywood displays a "Screen Show Ready to Begin" message and an OK button to start the show.

To save the show on disk, select Save Show on the Screen Show dialog box. Hollywood saves it with the same name as your presentation, unless you specify otherwise, but using an .HWS file extension rather than the standard .HWD. Make sure that both Compress Screen Show File and Device Independent Format are selected on the Screen Show dialog box, too. Creating the show will take a little longer, but the resulting file will be smaller, and you'll be able to display it on any computer that has Windows and the Screen Show program installed.

With the file saved, your show is now ready for an audience. Any time you're ready, simply select Screen Show on the Hollywood View menu, and then select Open on the Screen Show dialog box that appears. Select the screen show to display from the list and then select OK. Pass out the popcorn and no making out in the balcony. ★

9. Roll 'em!

Using Layers to Create a Complex Screen Show

▼

You set up progressive builds for text and data charts while you're still creating the chart. Then, when you show the chart in a screen show, you'll see it build step by step rather than appear all at once.

A screen show that uses effects to change pages is impressive. But even that can be bland compared to the show you can create taking advantage of Hollywood's layers.

Every Hollywood page is actually a pile of one hundred perfectly clear, transparent overlays, one on top of another. These overlays, called layers and numbered 0 to 99, are always present, whether you use them or not. You can place a drawing object or a chart object on any one of the hundred layers. If you ignore layers, Hollywood places everything you create on layer 0.

When you show a presentation page in a screen show, Hollywood reveals each layer you've drawn on one by one, gradually assembling a drawing or a chart step by step.

While you're creating the presentation, Hollywood offers you two ways to control which layer an object appears on. One is to select the object and then select a layer number for it with the Object Specs command on the View menu. The other way is to select the object and then use the Send to Layer command on the Layout menu, which lets you enter a layer number between 0 and 99.

After you've sent objects to different layers using Send to Layer or Object Specs, you can view single layers by clicking on ALL at the bottom of the presentation window

and then selecting a layer number from the list that appears. A second way is to use Show Layers on the Layout menu. Usually, Show Layers is set to show you all of the layers you've used on every page, but you also can enter a single layer or a range of consecutive layers to view. Now, as you turn from page to page in the presentation, you'll see only the objects on the selected layers.

If you use the Send to Layer or the Object Specs command, you'll be sending objects to different layers manually. This is helpful if you've drawn an illustration and want to reveal its different parts one at a time. But you can also have Hollywood automatically break apart your text or data charts and send the components to a range of layers, too. Later, when you display the page in a screen show, Hollywood shows the layers one at a time, seeming to reassemble the chart on the screen. This step-by-step building of charts is called a "progressive build." Whether or not a chart progressively builds is one of its options settings.

Progressively Building Text Charts

When you double-click on a text chart, one of the options you'll see in the dialog box is Progressive Build. Select this option and Hollywood automatically sends successive lines of text to a series of layers. For a table or tree chart, Progressive Build

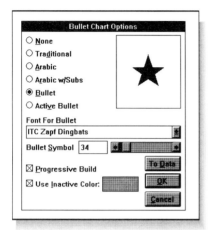

Progressive Build on the Bullet Chart Options dialog box makes new bulleted lines appear one by one. Use Inactive Color mutes the color of the old lines as new ones are added.

By Data Sets adds all the bars, lines, or slices in a series one series at a time. By Data Points adds the bars, lines, or slices of all series one at a time.

sends each of the *rows* to successive layers.

Active Bullet creates an interesting effect on a bullet chart. As you progress through the screen show, revealing first one layer and then the next, a single bullet seems to travel down the chart, appearing in front of each newly added line; that's because the bullet has been instructed to appear only on the newest layer added to the page.

Another option, Use Inactive Color, causes the text points you've already revealed in a progressive build to recede to a muted color, leaving only the newest point bright and prominent. To accomplish this, select Use Inactive Color in the dialog box and then select a muted color for Hollywood to use (click on the color panel next to this option).

Progressively Building Data Charts

Like the text points of a text chart, the bars, lines, or pie slices of a data chart can also be consecutively revealed.

Double-clicking on your chart gives you its options dialog box. When you select Series there, you'll see two Progressive Build options in the Series dialog box. One option, By Data Sets, automatically sends the different bars, lines, or pie slices to different layers. If your chart shows monthly sales figures for three different salesmen, you'll see the figures for each salesman appear one by one.

Another option, By Data Points, automatically sends each data point for all of the series to a different layer. In this case, the screen show would progressively reveal each month's sales figures for all three salesmen. ★

Selecting Transition Effects for Layers

Gradually revealing the layers that make up a page can be done simply or with flair, much like changing pages. It's all a question of the effects you choose for adding layers.

Now that you've separated your charts and illustrations onto layers — manually with the Send to Layer or Object Specs command, or automatically with Progressive Build — you're ready to specify the transition effects the screen show will use for revealing layers. You can, if you wish, specify a different transition effect for each and every layer on each and every page.

To begin specifying transition effects, turn to the first page in your presentation and then select Layers on the Layout menu. The Layers dialog box appears, showing a miniature of the first four layers on the page. You can use the scroll bar in the dialog box to scroll to still more layers.

Revealing Layers

To the right, under Show Layers, you can select one of three ways for this page's layers to be revealed: All at Once reveals all of the layers simultaneously, a single picture shown in one fell swoop; 1 at a Time shows each layer separately, one at a time, without showing the others; and Build lays down each successive layer on top of all the previous layers, slowly forming a composite. To gradually reveal a text or data chart,

you'll want to select Build.

The next step is to decide what kinds of effects you'd like Hollywood to use as it makes the transition from layer to layer. To make those choices, select More to expand the Layers dialog box.

To specify a different transition effect for each layer, select Chosen Layer at the Apply control, and then click on the first of the four miniatures showing a layer. Next, use the controls below — Effect, Speed, and Size — to select which transition effect to use, the speed of the transition, and the size of the effect; these are the same steps you took earlier when you selected transition effects for going from page to page. The choices you make here will govern how this layer reveals itself on the screen.

Now it's time to tell Hollywood just *when* to lay down the next layer. Under Timing, you can select Wait for Signal (if you'll be using a keyboard or mouse), or you can choose Show for __ Seconds and type in how long the layer should remain on the screen.

Once you've selected a transition effect for each layer, select OK. This brings you back to a view of the page in the main presentation window, and it binds your chosen effects to that page. You can now move on to the next page, and then the next, selecting transition effects as you wish. Later, when all your pages are incorporated into a screen show, the screen show will automatically display

---

You'll probably need to tinker with the transition times of layers until your charts appear on screen at the proper pace.

The transition effects are stored with the chart. Move the chart in the presentation, and the transition effects move, too.

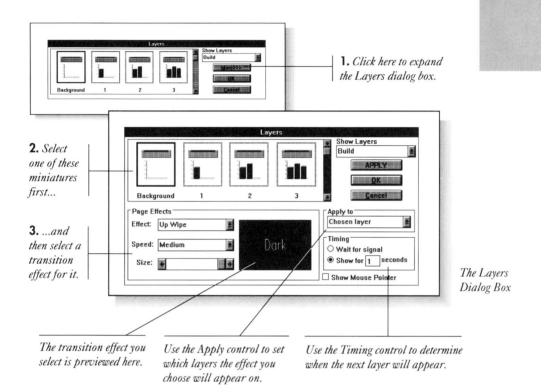

1. *Click here to expand the Layers dialog box.*

2. *Select one of these miniatures first...*

3. *...and then select a transition effect for it.*

The Layers Dialog Box

The transition effect you select is previewed here.

Use the Apply control to set which layers the effect you choose will appear on.

Use the Timing control to determine when the next layer will appear.

these transition effects — unless, of course, you choose Use Page Effects on the Screen Show dialog box to override the layer effects you've selected.

Transition effects don't have to be selected for each and every layer individually. The Apply control, where you found Chosen Layer, has two other settings you can use. All Layers lets you choose a transition effect and then automatically apply it to every layer on the page. The second, Chosen Layer to End, takes whatever transition effect you choose and applies it to the layer you're currently working on and to all the subsequent layers. ★

Here are special keystrokes and mouse button presses you can use to control a screen show.

Screen Show Controls

Right arrow/right mouse button	Move forward a layer
Left arrow/left mouse button	Move back a layer
Down arrow/double-click right mouse button	Move forward a page
Up arrow/double-click left mouse button	Move back a page
Esc	Stop the screen show
Home	Return to first page of screen show

Using the Screen Show Program

W ith your screen show created and saved on disk as an .HWS file, you could follow the instructions under "Running the Show" on page 165, but you don't really need Hollywood to show it. A special program called — what else? — Screen Show is really all you need. You'll find it on your hard disk, in the Hollywood directory, where the Hollywood installation process placed it.

Screen Show is a small Windows program that does nothing but run

Hollywood screen shows. If you'll be running your screen show on a computer other than the one you designed it on — one you travel with, say, or one belonging to a client — Screen Show is perfect. It's small and quick to load and takes up very little space on a hard disk. But, because it's a Windows application, the computer you run it on must be able to run Windows.

Another possibility is to run your screen show from a diskette — provided your .HWS file fits on a single diskette. Just copy the Screen Show program and your .HWS file onto the diskette, and it's Have Screen Show, Will Travel.

Starting the Screen Show Program

If you're showing your show with a computer that has Hollywood on it, you'll find the Screen Show program

in the same window of the Program Manager that has the Hollywood icon in it. The Screen Show icon looks like a little movie projector.

If you've copied both the Screen Show program and your screen show onto a diskette, you can use the Properties command on the File menu of the Windows Program Manager to configure the Screen Show icon so that it runs Screen Show from the floppy diskette. You also can use Run on the Windows Program Manager's File menu. Then, enter either A:SCRSHOW or B:SCRSHOW, depending on which disk drive the program is in.

When the Screen Show program starts, you'll see a blank screen and a single menu name: File. Under the File menu, you can use Open to bring up the Screen Show dialog box, the same dialog box you saw when you first created your screen show. Use Open on this dialog box and select the name of your screen show. As confirmation, the name of your screen show will appear at the top of the dialog box.

To start the show, select OK. Hollywood tells you, "Screen show is ready to begin." Click on OK again and the screen show starts.

Last-Minute Changes

Even as the curtain is set to rise, though, Hollywood lets you change your mind about a few things. Before you click on OK to start the show, you can overrule some of the choices you made back when you first created your show.

Say you've set up some elaborate layer effects and decide now you'd rather not use them; some simple page transition effects will do just fine. Selecting Use Page Effects ignores your layer effects, substituting the page effects you now specify in the Screen Show program. You can set one — sorry, just one — page effect that will govern every transition from page to page.

With the Show controls, you can make a final decision on which pages to include in the show and which to leave out. And you can change your mind about having the mouse pointer on screen to point things out with. Also available is the Repeat Until End Key control; select it now and the show will run continuously until the End key is pressed.

Notice, though, that the Preview control is grayed out and unavailable. Previewing is something you do only while you're still in Hollywood.

The Timing controls *are* still available. If you've set things up for each page to stay on the screen a specific length of time, it's not too late to tell them they've got to wait for a keystroke or mouse click instead. Or, of course, vice versa.

With all your changes in place, you're ready to choose OK to start the screen show, as above. The Screen Show program takes over now and displays your show full screen.

For a Happy Ending

When a screen show that runs automatically is finished, the Screen Show program's main screen automatically reappears. If you don't do something to prevent it, that's what you and your audience will find yourselves staring at as you reach your graceful conclusion.

The solution is simple. Make sure to use Wait for Signal on the last screen of your show, whether page or layer, so it will stay up on the screen until you've brought up the house lights, turned off the PC screen or projector, and told your audience, "That's all, folks." ★

Where To from Here?

✓ Outlining the Presentation
✓ Adding Bullet and Data Charts
✓ Adding Other Chart Types
✓ Adding the Trimmings: Extra Text and Graphics
✓ Formatting the Presentation
Next: Showing Off Your Work

Screen shows are one very dramatic way to show off the Hollywood presentations you've made. But you can also print your presentations or make slides. The next chapter covers these two methods of debuting your Hollywood feature.

The BIG PREMIERE

Producing Output

In This Chapter

◆

Using Presentation View

J ust as an artist stands back from his easel from time to time to gain perspective on his work, you also can get a wide-angle look at your presentation, using Hollywood's Presentation View. Presentation View shows nine miniature pages at a time, neatly arranged in little boxes on the screen.

The miniatures in Presentation View, called "thumbnails" (as in thumbnail sketches), won't let you see much detail. They're so small that you usually can't make out much text. But you will be able to see charts and you should be able to read page titles, at least well enough to tell which page is which. And that's all you need to make Presentation View work for you.

Presentation View lets you do a final check on a presentation to be sure everything looks right. You'll be able to see, for example, if a title is out of place or a chart is hanging off a page. You'll also be able to confirm that all pages have a uniform look, and that the color scheme has successfully done its job.

Presentation View also helps you navigate through a presentation. Can't remember which page shows that pie chart of regional sales? Use Presentation View to find it, and then double-click on the page to jump directly to it.

Most people will use Presentation View as a slide sorter, though, to shuffle pages around within a presentation. You can simply drag a page from one position to another on the Presentation View screen, changing the order of pages, even at the last minute. You'll particularly appreciate the ease of checking and shuffling pages destined for a screen show, since, unlike printed pages or 35mm slides, with a screen show the progression stored on disk is the progression your audience will see; there'll be no shuffling slides or prints in your lap at the last minute.

Bringing up Presentation View

Switching to Presentation View is easy. Simply select Presentation from the View menu. In a moment you'll see your first nine pages appear in the Presentation View window. If your presentation has more than nine pages, use the scroll bar in the window to scroll through the rest.

To move a page, simply click on it and drag it to a new position. When you move a page on top of an existing page, the existing page and all of the pages that follow it move back in the presentation to make room.

To view any single page in the main presentation window, double-click on its thumbnail.

Copying and Cutting Charts in Presentation View

The commands at the bottom of the Presentation View window let you cut unwanted pages and make duplicates of pages you particularly

---

Presentation View lets you stand back from a presentation and get an overall view.

Presentation View is also a great way to find a page in your presentation that's eluding you.

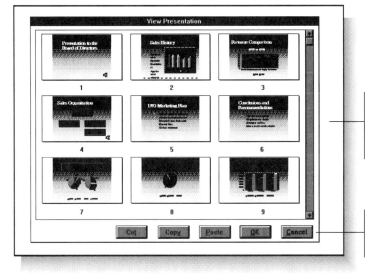

Double-click on any page to jump right to that page full screen.

Simply drag pages from one position to another to move them in the presentation order....

...or select a page and then click on one of these buttons to cut or copy it.

Presentation View

like. First, you click on the page you wish to cut or copy. Then, to delete the page, select Cut. Hollywood removes the page and closes up the hole in the presentation. To copy a page, click on it and select Copy. Then, click where the page should go and select Paste. You'll get a duplicate of the page at the new position.

To abandon the changes you've made and return to the original presentation order, select Cancel. To proceed with all of your changes intact, select OK instead. You'll be returned to the main view of a single page. ★

Duplicating Page Designs in Presentation View

Presentation View can be especially handy when you want to pattern a new page after a page design you already have and like. Imagine that part of a presentation will be a series of pie charts. Set up one page with a pie chart just the way you want it, and then use Copy within

Presentation View to make as many duplicates as you need. Now, you can return to each duplicate page and simply change the data in each pie chart's data table. Change the page titles in the Outliner, if necessary, hit Draw Chart, and you're done.

Printing a Presentation

Printing the pages you've created in Hollywood is easy. All you have to do is press Ctrl-P and then Enter to send every page in your presentation to the current printer set up under Windows. Or, you can select Print on the File menu. To print only certain pages, select From in the Print dialog box that appears and then enter starting and ending page numbers. To print just one page, enter its number in both the From and To text boxes of the Print dialog box. The printers you see listed at the bottom of the Print dialog box are those that are currently available under Windows. To select a different printer, use Change Printer on the File menu. This takes you to the printer selection controls on the Windows Control Panel. Use the Control Panel to select a new printer and then close or minimize the Control Panel window so you can return to Hollywood.

To be certain printing is really as easy for you as simply selecting Print, you must remember to do a bit of advance work, back when you first start a Hollywood presentation. That's the time to check the preference file to make sure that both the Page Format and the Output Device are correct. Remember, Hollywood uses the current preference file to configure each new presentation you begin. The settings for Page Format and Output Device determine how Hollywood will set up your presentation's basic page. If you know in advance that you'll be creating slides, you should be sure you're using a preference file that sets Page Format to 35mm Slide. If you're planning to print pages you'll duplicate onto overhead transparencies, make sure the preference file specifies Overhead as the Page Format.

▼

To be sure you get just what you expect when you print a presentation, make sure the Page Format and Output Device settings are appropriate to your printer, plotter, or slide recorder.

Exporting a Page to a File

You may find you like one of your Hollywood charts or illustrations so much that you wish you could include it in a memo or newsletter. You can. Hollywood lets you export individual presentation pages to graphics files that you can then import into a word processor or desktop publishing package for printing. Just get the page you want to export on the screen, and then use the Export Page As command on the File menu. Select one of the available export file types and then type in a name for the file before selecting OK. You'll learn all about the export file formats supported by Hollywood in Chapter 11.

As you learned in Chapter 8, even after you've begun work on your presentation, it's still possible to override the Page Format and Output Device settings by using the Page Setup command. But that's likely to yield surprising results. If you change the Page Format setting, Hollywood will indeed change the size and shape of the basic page accordingly, but the charts, text, and graphic objects you've placed on the pages will remain the same size. Change from a Page Format setting of Screen to a new setting of Overhead, for example, and Hollywood creates a much larger page but your charts remain the same size, so they end up in the upper left corner, looking small on the new, larger page. Another way to think about this is to remember that the Object Specs settings for the objects remain the same no matter what Page Format setting you use.

Simply checking the Page Format and Output Device settings back when you're still looking at a blank Hollywood page will save you trouble later.

Clipping vs. Scaling

If you try to print a landscape (sideways) page with a printer that's been set up for portrait (upright) printing, Hollywood may not be able to fit the entire screen page onto the printed page. If it can't, it will ask you whether to "Clip" the output or "Scale" it. Clipping cuts off the portion that won't fit. Scaling reduces the overall size of the screen page to fit on the printed page. The text and graphic objects won't be the size you originally specified, but the entire image will fit nicely on the page. ★

Steps to Assure Good Printing

1. When you begin a presentation, use Page Format and Output Device settings that are appropriate for your expected output device. The easiest way to assure this is by using a preference file that has stored the correct settings.
2. Be sure you've selected the correct printer and the correct output port with the Windows Control Panel. You can get to the Control Panel by selecting Change Printer on the File menu. The selected printer will be highlighted in the lower portion of Hollywood's Print dialog box.
3. Make sure the setup for the printer is correct (Landscape vs. Portrait, Automatic feed vs. Manual feed, etc.) in the Windows Control Panel.

Making Slides

You can expect stunning slides from MAGICorp, if you give them a stunning Hollywood presentation design to reproduce.

MAGICorp can also create color laser prints, color transparencies, and photographic prints from your Hollywood pages.

Hollywood comes equipped with a special program that can take a file full of slides you've created and send it by telephone to MAGICorp, a slide-making company in suburban New York. You won't have to pay for a long-distance call to New York, because MAGICorp has its own toll-free 800 number. If you send the slide file to MAGICorp before noon, your slides will be finished that very afternoon and on their way back to you via Airborne's overnight delivery service. You'll get them the following day, or within forty-eight hours if you opt for MAGICorp's economy service.

The slides MAGICorp produces are absolutely stunning. They're perfectly faithful renditions of exactly what you've created on the screen, except they look even better, for two reasons. First, they have very high resolution. Slides in general have much higher resolution than printed output. Second, MAGICorp's slide makers have an extremely broad color palette, so color washes especially look stunning. You'll never see the transition point from one shade of a color to the next; they just seem to blend seamlessly.

From the same file, MAGICorp can also print color overhead transparencies, color laser pages, and color prints. You can even specify by number one of MAGICorp's Showstopper backgrounds for the

pages of your presentation. The selection includes a variety of marbles, granites, woods, and topical images, such as flags and city skylines. MAGICorp will send you an information packet about its service and about its Showstopper backgrounds.

Preparing a Slide File

When you first install Hollywood, you have the option to install the MAGICorp files. If you go ahead and install them, you'll then find a special MAGICorp printer driver when you try to select an output device, and in the Hollywood window of the Windows Program Manager you'll find the MAGIComm communications program for sending your files to MAGICorp's 800 number.

Before you begin a presentation that you plan to send to MAGICorp, you must select the proper preference file — either MAGICorp Slides or MAGICorp Shwstopper — so that the presentation starts with the correct Page Format and Output Device settings. If you don't have the proper preference file already set up, you can use the Page Setup command, selecting 35mm Slides as the Page Format and Magicorp Slide Service as the Output Device.

Among your predesigned color schemes you'll find several that have been provided for use with the MAGICorp service. These have been professionally crafted to give you

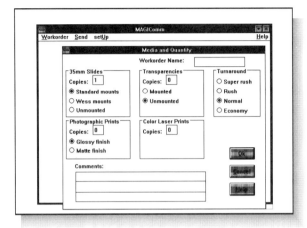

Sending slides to MAGICorp is just a matter of printing the slide file and then filling out a few forms in the MAGIComm communications program.

beautiful results. You may, if you choose, use your own color scheme, though. MAGICorp can reproduce anything you can make on the Hollywood screen.

If you choose to have MAGICorp create and mount your slides, don't forget that you'll need to leave about a quarter-inch border around each page to make room for the cardboard mount.

Finally, before printing, use Change Printer on the File menu, and select Magicorp Slide Service on FILE:. Now, when you print the presentation, Hollywood will ask for a filename and will save the presentation on disk with the extension .SLI.

To send the .SLI file to MAGICorp by modem, start the MAGIComm communications program by double-clicking on its icon in the Windows Program Manager. Next, use the Workorder menu in the MAGIComm

program's window to put your presentation file on the transmission list and to fill out your requirements for the job. Finally, use the commands on the Send menu to send the transmission list and job information to MAGICorp.

Before you can use MAGICorp the first time, you must contact the company to set up an account. Call 1-800-367-6244, or use the order form you'll find inside your Hollywood package.

Using an Agfa Matrix Film Recorder

Rather than sending your slides out to be made, you can make your own if you have access to an Agfa Matrix film recorder. To export pages for a film recorder, use the Export Page command and select SCODL as the export format. ★

Printing Notes and Handout Pages

If you're the one who'll give the presentation, you can enter your notes on Notes pages with the Text tool. Otherwise, you can leave the text area blank under the slide miniature for the speaker to make his or her own notes.

Only world-class presentation graphics packages — Hollywood included, of course — let you produce two kinds of supporting material to accompany a presentation: speaker's notes and presentation handouts. One helps you; the other helps your audience.

Making Speaker's Notes

After you've finished a presentation, you may want to prepare a separate set of pages, called notes pages, for use by the person who will be giving the presentation. Each notes page displays a miniature of a presentation page at the top, leaving a large blank area below. Using the Text tool, you can type speaker's notes into the blank area while you're still preparing the presentation, or you can add the notes later with a typewriter. Of course, if you yourself will be the speaker, you can always scribble in your notes by hand, but beware of trying to make out your own handwriting while simultaneously trying keeping your composure in front of an audience.

To create notes pages, make sure you've got the presentation on the screen and then select Notes Pages from the View menu. You'll see a miniature of the current page on the upper portion of a page. Click on the chart and you'll see that it has frame handles you can use to resize the chart or move it to a new location on

the notes page.

Below the chart will be the blank area for your notes. To type notes in using the Text tool, select the Regular Text tool from the Text drawer of the Toolbox and then draw a large rectangle with it that almost completely fills the lower portion of the screen. Now, you can type into the rectangle. When your text reaches the right side of the rectangle as you type, it will word wrap to the next line. Then, advance to the next page as you do normally in Hollywood and create the next notes page.

Generating Presentation Handouts

Each printed handout page displays up to six of your charts in miniature. With handout pages, you can condense a twelve-slide presentation onto two handout pages. Distributing handout pages gives your audience something to refer to during the presentation and afterwards — and, of course, something to shuffle around noisily while you're trying to be heard.

The number of presentation pages you display on each handout page is determined using the Pages Per Handout setting on the Page Setup dialog box. Page Setup is under the File menu. The available choices are one, two, three, four, or six presentation pages on each handout page. The Pages Per Handout setting also appears on the Preferences dialog

People love anything that's free. Passing out handout pages is the quickest way to win over an audience.

box so it can be set as a default for all your presentations.

When you have a presentation on the screen and you select Handout Page from the View menu, you'll see a miniature of a chart in a white area on the screen. The rest of the page, where the other charts will be, is covered by gray.

Unfortunately, while assembling a handout page you can see only a single page on the screen at a time. Even if a handout page will have four charts printed on it, you'll see only one at a time, each in its own area of the page surrounded by gray. To see the next chart on the page, turn the page using the right arrow at the bottom of the window, just as you normally do in Hollywood.

You may find that each miniature

page on the handout page does not completely fill its portion of the handout page (the white area surrounded by gray). When you click directly on one of the page miniatures, you'll see that it becomes surrounded by handles that you can use to increase its size or to drag it to a new position within its space on the page.

You can print either notes or handout pages just as you would normal Hollywood presentation pages. While either Notes Pages or Handout Pages is selected on the Layout menu, select Print on the File menu to send your pages to a printer. ★

Where To from Here?

✓ Outlining the Presentation
✓ Adding Bullet and Data
    Charts
✓ Adding Other Chart Types
✓ Adding the Trimmings: Extra
    Text and Graphics
✓ Formatting the Presentation
✓ Showing Off Your Work

That's it. You've got your presentation. You can stop here. Hey! Not so fast. Take a look at the goodies in the last chapter before you finish up. You'll find lots of little things that simply didn't fit well anywhere else in the book.

EXTRAS

In This Chapter

◆

Creating Custom Toolboxes

B y now, you've seen that nearly everything about Hollywood can be customized. So it shouldn't surprise you to learn that even toolboxes themselves can be custom built. Custom toolboxes are just one more way for you to put your personal stamp on Hollywood.

With Hollywood's Get Toolbox command, on the Layout menu, you can rearrange the Hollywood Toolbox, moving tools from drawer to drawer, getting rid of tools you'll never use, or even splitting the Toolbox into two separate toolboxes, each with a different set of tools. Everyone in the office can even set up an individual toolbox labeled with a special name and incorporated into his or her own preference file.

Before you start tinkering with the arrangement of the Toolbox, though, take a look at the sensible way it's arranged. The tools in the standard toolbox that comes from the factory are neatly separated into drawers by function. In the Data Charts drawer, you'll find all the tools you need for creating data charts. In the Draw drawer, you'll find all the tools you need to draw shapes on the screen. And so on.

You may find, though, that you have no use for some tools. Perhaps you'll never need high-low-close charts. Or perhaps the only text charts you'll create with Hollywood are bullet charts — no table or tree charts needed, thank you. Maybe it'll suit you to rearrange the Toolbox, fitting more tools into fewer drawers and thereby reducing the size of the Toolbox on the screen. With the Get Toolbox command on the Layout menu, you can customize Hollywood's Toolbox any way you'd like.

Your Own Handy Toolbox

To modify the Toolbox or create your own, select Get Toolbox on the Layout menu. Until you make your own custom toolboxes, the Get Toolbox dialog box that appears shows only one toolbox (Tools). To customize this toolbox and make your own, select New. In a moment, you'll see the Build Toolbox dialog box,

Have your Toolbox on the screen when you create a preference file, and loading the preference file will always load your Toolbox, too.

Creating an Outline Drawer

While you're still learning Hollywood, you may have difficulty finding your way to Hollywood's Outliner. You get there by selecting the Bullet Chart tool in the Text Charts drawer — but that just may not seem intuitive.

As a navigational tool, you may wish to combine the tools from two drawers into one — say, Paint and Crop — and then label the emptied drawer "Outline." In this drawer, you'd place a second copy of the Bullet Chart tool. Now, you can click on the Outline drawer to jump to the Outliner immediately.

which lists the drawer names of the Toolbox that comes with Hollywood. Beside each name are eight positions for tools. The tools that are already in each drawer occupy the first several positions. The other, still-blank positions are filled with gray.

To move a tool from one drawer to another, simply drag it from its position in one drawer to a position in another. To remove a tool from a drawer, drag it anyplace outside the confines of the dialog box. To add a tool that you don't already have in any drawer, select it from the scrollable list to the right and then click on a position for it. To rename a drawer, simply double-click on its name and then type another name in its place.

If you double-click on a drawer name and then press the Del key to delete the name, plus leave all eight positions next to it empty, Hollywood will remove that drawer from the toolbox altogether when you save the revised toolbox. This way, you can combine tools in drawers and make a smaller toolbox if you want.

When you finish customizing a toolbox, replace the current toolbox name in the upper right corner of the dialog box with a new name and then select Save. To leave the Build Toolbox dialog box and return to the prior dialog box (Get Toolbox), select OK. Then, select OK again in the Get Toolbox dialog box to see the new toolbox on the screen. To remove an old toolbox still on the screen, double click on its control button (at its upper left corner). ★

Give Your Presentation a Sound Track!

It's like turning an old silent movie into a talkie. Simply by copying a small $98 program, called PC-Sound™, into your Hollywood directory, you can add a brand-new tool to Hollywood's collection. Select the Sound tool and then click on a page and the PC-Sound dialog box lets you select prerecorded digital sound clips that will automatically play whenever the page appears in a screen show. PC-Sound comes with a little device that snaps onto your PC's parallel port that sends crisp, clear sound to an external amplifier (perhaps the audio system in a meeting room). With a separate accessory, called PC-Recorder™ you can even record your own sound — perhaps a voice-over from the chairman of the company for a stockholders' meeting. To learn more about PC-Sound, contact Arkay Technologies, Inc., 5 Tsienneto Road, Suite 2, Derry, NH 03038; phone (800) 786-2419.

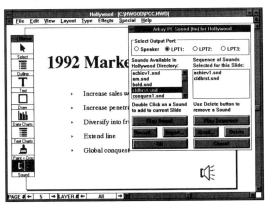

Exporting Hollywood Pages

You export an
entire Hollywood
page to a file.
After you import
the file into a
desktop
publishing or
word processing
program, you
can crop out the
portion you don't
want.

Hollywood is a
superb tool for
preparing charts
and graphs for
printed docu-
ments.

Hollywood makes sensational presentations, stunning screen shows, and smashing slides, but you can also use it to create the charts, special text logos, and drawings you need for your company newsletter, brochure, proposal, or other printed document.

A special command on the File menu, Export Page As, lets you export a complete Hollywood page into a graphic file on disk. You can then import that file into another program, for word processing or desktop publishing.

If you'll be using a Windows application to create your printed documents, then translating charts and graphs from Hollywood is particularly easy. Hollywood can export Windows metafiles, TIFF, or PCX images that are then easily imported into Microsoft Word for Windows, Aldus PageMaker, or Ventura Publisher for Windows, among others. You can also transfer graphics from Hollywood to another Windows application through the Windows Clipboard. You'll learn about both of these methods in a minute.

If you're using a non-Windows application to create printed documents, such as WordPerfect, Microsoft Word, or IBM's new word processor, Signature, you can import Hollywood files into that application just as easily. Hollywood can export to a file in any one of thirteen

different graphics file formats. Surely your software can import at least one of them.

From Hollywood to Another Windows Program

Transferring a Hollywood page to another Windows application is a snap. You can export it as a Windows metafile (the instructions for that appear below), or you can simply cut or copy a graphic in Hollywood and transfer it to the Windows Clipboard. Once the graphic is on the Clipboard, you can open another Windows application and then use Paste to bring it into your document.

To export a Windows metafile, while you're still in Hollywood bring to the screen the page you want to export. Now select Export Page As on the File menu. On the Export Page As dialog box, you can choose one of thirteen output file formats. Select Windows Metafile, and then type a filename into the Name text box. Hollywood automatically appends the proper .WMF file extension to the filename.

If you will be printing your document with a PostScript printer, or sending the document to a high-resolution PostScript imagesetter, you'll get superb quality by exporting an Encapsulated PostScript file (.EPS). Unfortunately, Hollywood does not include a bit-mapped image of your page in the .EPS file, which means you won't be able to see a

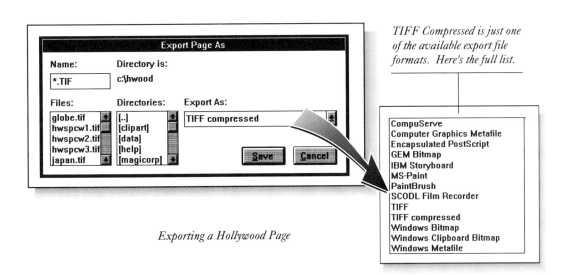

CompuServe
Computer Graphics Metafile
Encapsulated PostScript
GEM Bitmap
IBM Storyboard
MS-Paint
PaintBrush
SCODL Film Recorder
TIFF
TIFF compressed
Windows Bitmap
Windows Clipboard Bitmap
Windows Metafile

Exporting a Hollywood Page

screen representation of the page in a desktop publishing program.

Exporting a page as a TIFF file (Tagged Image File Format) creates a file you can easily pull into virtually any desktop publishing program. If your program can accept compressed TIFF files (PageMaker can import them, for example), select TIFF Compressed as the export file format. This will create a smaller TIFF file and save disk space. If you plan to import a Hollywood chart into the GEM version of Ventura Publisher, choose GEM Bitmap to create an .IMG file. The GEM version of Ventura Publisher translates all bit-mapped files you import to .IMG files anyway.

Choosing an Appropriate Color Scheme

To assure the best possible results in your word processing or desktop publishing program, you should use a color scheme in Hollywood that's suited for the eventual output device you'll be using. For example, if you'll be printing the output of your word processor or desktop publishing program with a black-and-white HP LaserJet, be sure to use a color scheme that assigns black, white, and shades of gray to objects. If, on the other hand, you'll be using a color printer, you can use one of the color schemes that incorporates color. ★

Tips and Tricks

H ere are a few tips and tricks you can use to make Hollywood work better.

Tips and Tricks are something we all find as we use any program more and more.

Duplicating Page Designs in Presentation View

Hollywood does a superb job of creating the charts you need, but placing them on the page is up to you. When you happen across a page design you especially like, you can recycle the design by duplicating the page in Presentation View and then changing its contents.

For example, if you're creating a series of charts that are all the same except for the data, you can get the first one just the way you want it, and then, using Copy, duplicate the page it's on several times. Now you can go from page to page and simply change the data in the data table that underlies each chart.

One Presentation, Several Master Designs

Normally, you'd use the Master Page to apply the same design elements to every page in your presentation: a company logo, for example. But say you're giving a two-part presentation, each part focusing on a different company or organization. You could create two basic page designs, one for each half of the presentation. Here's how: Create only the first page of your presentation and place on it the first organization's logo plus whatever

design elements you want. Then, in Presentation View, use Copy to duplicate the page as many times as you need for the first part of the presentation. Next, create a new page following the duplicated pages, this time using the second logo and a different graphic design, and duplicate this one as many times as you need to finish the presentation. Now go ahead and add text and data charts to all the pages.

Replacing Bullet Chart Titles with Special Text

It's a little bit of extra work, but you may want to replace the page titles that came from the Outliner with titles made of special text. One advantage of special text is that you can put a shadow behind it. Especially if you're creating slides, a subtle shadow behind the page title can give a page real pizzazz.

Use a Font Manager to Add Extra Regular Text Fonts

A font manager like Adobe Type Manager or Bitstream Facelift can instantly add new text fonts to Windows. Once you've added new fonts to Windows, they'll also show up in Hollywood's list of fonts for regular text. Both Adobe and Bitstream sell inexpensive font collections that will give a Hollywood user the same full set of fonts found in most PostScript printers.

I'd love to hear about the tips and tricks you discover. Come join the IBM Desktop Software forum on CompuServe (Go IBMDESK). You'll find me hanging out there. (72456,3325)

Use Regular Text in Styles for Text Rather than Special Text Fonts

Hollywood draws text on the screen faster when you avoid using Swiss 721 and Dutch 801. This is particularly helpful when you're working with a lot of text in the Data Manager or the Outliner. So, when you use Define Styles to set styles for the Data Manager and Outliner, specify regular Windows fonts or fonts generated by a font manager instead.

Create Different Styles for Denser and Looser Bullet Charts

A Hollywood color scheme designates only one text style for all the bulleted lines of text in a presentation. But some bullet charts have more subtitles in them than others and, for appearance's sake, may need more space between the lines. To do that, you can create different styles for the bullet chart subtitles on different pages. For those pages with few bulleted text lines, use a style that has lots of extra lead (extra space) between lines to spread them out. For pages with many bulleted text lines, use a style that has little extra lead to fit them all in.

Ideas for Making Hollywood Faster

There are times when Hollywood might move a little slower than you'd like. But there are a few steps you can take, short of buying a faster computer system, to give Hollywood a shot in the arm.

☆ First, use SmartDrive (provided with Windows and usually installed by Windows) or another disk cache to speed up your hard disk. Hollywood, like most Windows applications, uses the disk drive often while it works.

☆ If you're using an 80386 computer, try running Windows in Standard mode rather than in Enhanced mode. Start Windows by typing WIN /S rather than just WIN. DOS applications that you run in Windows won't continue to execute in the background when you switch to Hollywood, but your Windows applications will probably run noticeably faster.

☆ Make sure you've got plenty of memory in your system. These days memory is inexpensive. You should have at least four megabytes of memory. Reserve the first megabyte exclusively for SmartDrive.

☆ Use a fast, 16-bit VGA or SuperVGA card. Everything will appear on the screen faster.

Connect with IBM's Desktop Software Forum on CompuServe

IBM has its own forum on CompuServe (IBMDESK), with a special message base for conversation about Hollywood and a special data library reserved exclusively for files for Hollywood. You're likely to get quick answers to your questions, pick up lots of useful information from the Hollywood experts hanging around, and find lots of sample files and demonstration versions of new software that works with Hollywood. When you log on, leave a message for me (72456,3325). I'd love to hear about your major Hollywood productions! ★

PC Coordinator's Guide to Hollywood

If your job is to ease the path for other computer users in your office or workgroup, then you're going to love Hollywood. With this one program you can satisfy the power users in your group, who'll thrive on the richness and flexibility of its drawing and charting tools, as well as the more casual users, who want something that's "smart" enough to generate attractive, professional-looking presentations almost on its own. These users will never dig deep enough into the program to learn all that Hollywood can do. All they want are results without fuss, and Hollywood can deliver them.

Rather than frustrate one group of users or the other by being either too sophisticated or too simplified, Hollywood can keep its more involved features (color schemes and templates, for example) neatly tucked away. They're always available for those with the inclination to learn, but they can be totally automated for those who'd rather just plug in words and numbers and have Hollywood spit out finished, masterful presentations.

To make Hollywood almost completely automatic, though, you'll need to do a little advance work before your users get their hands on the program — not much, but enough to be sure Hollywood is customized for the equipment you've got on hand and for the type of presentations your users are likely to make. If you've anticipated both of these correctly, then you can make Hollywood virtually foolproof. Your users will love you for it.

Here are some ideas for automating Hollywood:

Setting Up Preference Files

For each different type of presentation your users will create, set up one preference file. For the overheads they'll print on a laser printer, for example, set up a preference file that automatically selects the Overhead page format, uses a laser printer color scheme, and specifies a laser printer as the output device. Then, instruct your users to: (1) select the appropriate preference file for their presentation, and (2) select New on the File menu to start a new presentation rather than beginning work directly on the blank page they see when they first start up Hollywood. In the preference file, you might want to select Last Saved Presentation for On Startup Load. This way, your users *must* select New to begin a new presentation.

When you set up a preference file, you can also establish the defaults for each of Hollywood's tools (usually, you press Ctrl when you select a tool to establish its defaults), you can arrange Hollywood's windows on the screen, and you can select one of the toolboxes you've previously customized. If your users will never create high-low-close charts or Bezier curves, you may want to remove the

High-low-close tool from the Data Charts drawer of the Toolbox and delete the Bezier Curve tool from the Draw drawer. Removing these tools and placing this modified toolbox in a preference file will give your users two less things to worry about.

You might even consider setting up different preference files for different users. If Eric, the sales rep, always creates color overheads on a color laser printer, why not set him up with a preference file that selects a color scheme and page format suited to the color laser printer.

Now, with preference files established just the way your users will need them, rather than leave Hollywood's full set of preference files on the system, delete those you don't need to narrow the choices your users will have to face.

Weeding Out Inappropriate Color Schemes

Hollywood comes with a broad selection of color schemes, many of which are optimized for particular output devices. You may want to remove those color schemes that won't work well with the output devices you have on hand. If you use a standard HP LaserJet rather than a PostScript printer, for example, or if you don't have a fancy Tektronix color printer, you may want to remove the PostScript and Tektronix color schemes from the list.

Creating Templates for Different Presentation Types

Another useful way to customize Hollywood is to set up a simple selection of template files from which your users can choose. Eliminate those that are meant for output devices you don't have. Create a selection of additional templates that are suited both to the types of presentations your users give and to the output devices you have available. If your corporate standard specifies certain colors, certain fonts, and the corporate logo at a designated position on the page, make these changes to all of your templates.

You may want to group together all the templates designed for a particular output device, placing each group in a different subdirectory under the templates subdirectory. Then, when a user needs a template for a screen show, for example, he or she can look in the screen show template subdirectory.

Remember, template files not only call up a color scheme, but they also automatically position on the page the charts your users create. Therefore, instruct your users that every time they create a presentation they should: (1) first select a preference file appropriate for the intended output, and (2) select from the templates one that matches the output device and that institutes a presentation design they like. Now, as they use the Outliner to create a series of bullet chart pages and add other text charts and data charts, each chart will fall into place. What's more, the entire presentation will have the elements the template has placed on the Master Page and the color scheme the template has chosen. ★

Index

◆

About the Author

Steve Sagman has written the best-seller *Using Harvard Graphics* and *1-2-3 Graphics Techniques*. He writes about personal computers, particularly presentation graphics, in *PC/Computing*, *PC Week*, and *PC Magazine*. His company creates courseware and user documentation, and it provides training and consulting services. Please contact the author at the address listed below for information about both traditional and on-line Hollywood training and courseware that can accompany this book.

Contacting the Author

A book is never really finished. Each new edition is augmented by the experiences of its readers. The author would be grateful for your feedback, too.

He is best reached on electronic mail via:
MCI Mail (SSAGMAN), or
CompuServe (72456,3325).

You may also write:
Steve Sagman
140 Charles St.
New York, NY 10014

Colophon

This book was written with Microsoft Word for Windows and published with PC PageMaker 4.0. Screens were captured with HotShot Graphics and Collage Plus, and then individually color corrected for optimal printing. Hollywood sample pages were exported directly from Hollywood as compressed TIFF files or as Windows Metafiles and imported into PageMaker. Silhouette illustrations were scanned as line art. Body type is Caslon 540 and Caslon 3. Other type is Bauer Bodoni Bold Condensed and Futura Medium. The cover was designed and produced using traditional graphic arts methods.

Finished pages were sent to ACT Graphics of Cranford, NJ who did a masterful job imagesetting them on an Agfa Matrix imagesetter.